CONNOISSEUR'S LIBRARY

THE LOUIS STYLES
Louis XIV, Louis XV, Louis XVI

NIETTA APRÀ

WORLD PUBLISHING
TIMES MIRROR
NEW YORK

Contents

3   Louis XIV, the Sun King
3   A great minister
4   Charles Le Brun
4   Gobelins, Beauvais and Aubusson
5   The palaces and royal châteaux
6   André-Charles Boulle, master cabinet-maker
6   The Sun King's throne
7   A new regime
7   Louis XV, 'le roi bien-aimé'
8   Louis XV furniture
11   The downfall of the rocaille
11   The royal porcelain
12   Louis XVI: 'too young to reign'
12   A change in style
13   Beds, chairs and silks
14   Papiers-peints
16   Index of artists

The photographs in this book were taken by:
C. Ciccione (4, 8, 15); G. Dagli Orti (1, 2, 6, 7, 12, 16–21,
28–35, 37–39, 41–45, 54–59, 62–65, 69, 70, 75–82, 84,
86–90, 92–96); John Freeman (3, 9–11, 13, 14, 23–27, 46,
52, 53, 60, 61, 67, 68, 71–73, 85, 91). The line drawings are
by Mario Logli.

Translated from the Italian of Nietta Aprà

Published by The World Publishing Company
First American edition
First printing—1973
Copyright © Istituto Geografico De Agostini, Novara 1970
Translation © Orbis Publishing Limited, London 1972
All rights reserved
ISBN 0-529-05016-1
Library of Congress catalog card number: 72-10447
Phototypeset in England by Petty and Sons Limited, Leeds
Printed in Italy by IGDA, Novara

Library of Congress cataloging in publication data

Aprà, Nietta.
   The Louis styles.

   (Connoisseur's library)
   1. Furniture, French—History. 2. Decoration and ornament—
Louis XIV style. 3. Decoration and ornament—Louis XV style.
4. Decoration and ornament—Louis XVI style. I. Title. II. Series:
Connoisseur's library (New York)
NK2548.A69   749.2′4   72-10447
ISBN 0-529-05016-1

WORLD PUBLISHING
TIMES MIRROR

Louis XIV,
the Sun King

The Louis XIV style was the fruit of the combined efforts of three strong personalities: first, that most autocratic of monarchs, Louis XIV; secondly, the great minister, Jean-Baptiste Colbert; and thirdly, a gifted painter, Charles Le Brun. The aim towards which the life and work of these three men was directed was that of enhancing the *grandeur du Roi*, of creating in seventeenth-century France the pomp and splendour that was to be epitomized by the name Louis XIV; together their boundless energy had a profound influence in every branch of the decorative arts. As his emblem, the King chose a blazing sun – whence his name of *Roi Soleil*, or Sun King – and as a motto the phrase 'L'état c'est moi, le Roi gouverne par lui-même' ('I am the state, the King alone rules').

Louis XIV carried this motto into practice by fostering a cult of distant majesty about him, imposing on his subjects the most rigid and immutable rules of etiquette. Even such mundane everyday activities as getting up, eating, walking, hunting or going to bed at night, became public affairs whose every detail was minutely planned and regulated. The famous ceremony of the *lever du Roi* is an example; the King would get out of bed in the presence of at least a hundred courtiers, of whom the most privileged were admitted at the very moment when the King deigned to put a royal foot to the floor and don a dressing gown. Others, less fortunate, were permitted to be present only for the few moments it took the King to wipe his hands on a spirit-soaked towel. (This was all the washing he did.) There was the solemn presentation of the Royal shirt, brought on a white silk cushion by the Dauphin or a prince of the blood; the right sleeve was held by the first *valet de chambre*, the left by the *valet de garde-robe*. The master of ceremonies then had the honour of helping the King put on his breeches.

In the same way, the ceremonies surrounding the meals that the King took alone in his room were no less solemn and reverential. On the days of the *grand couvert*, the public was allowed to be present at His Majesty's repast, and the King, always enthroned alone at his table, would have at least thirty people around, not counting the sixteen armed guards and the Alms-giver. The office of *Grand Maître de France* in charge of the King's table was always given to the first prince of the blood, the Prince de Condé. The sense of majesty and attention to detail displayed in such ceremonies characterized the everyday life of King and Court, and was in turn to be seen reflected in everything that surrounded them, from palaces and gardens to interiors and their furnishing: a style, in fact, that is simply known as 'Louis XIV'.

A great minister

The second great personality in our story, Jean-Baptiste Colbert, (1619–1683), began his career under this autocratic King, and was his greatest minister. At various times, Colbert held the offices of Controller General of Finance, Secretary of the Navy, Secretary of Industry, and Secretary of the Royal Household. An indefatigable administrator, often working 16 hours a day, he used to enter his office at five-thirty in the morning. It is reported too, by contemporaries, that at the sight of his desk covered in papers he would rub his hands in satisfaction, getting down to work with the zeal of a gourmet approaching a banquet of tempting dishes.

The Ministry of Fine Arts was one of the nine over which Colbert presided during his years in office. He was responsible for developing its potential beyond all previous bounds, stimulating the existing silk and textile industries, founding new factories to manufacture goods that France lacked and which, until then, had been imported. Establishments such as the Royal factory of Saint-Gobain, which made glass, formerly imported from Venice, the Gobelins factory, and the Aubusson and Beauvais factories were all set up by Colbert. By its own efforts Lyons became one of the most important centres for silks and textiles, while other textile factories sprang up at Abbeville, Sedan and Carcassonne. The towns of Alençon, Chantilly and Le Havre became important centres for lace-making and embroidery products, which until then had been brought from Malines and Venice.

Not only did Colbert try to cut down the imports of foreign goods, however; he also made an effort to expand the market for French goods abroad. In an inflexible and authoritarian manner he personally controlled every branch of craft and industry as he strove to make French products the best, and the most sought-after in Europe. It was Colbert himself who laid down the rules that minutely governed the breadth and length of cloth, and the number of threads in the warp and weft, as well as the processes used for making dyes. Further regulations and edicts issued by him required every worker to identify his work by signing it; any piece deemed imperfect by the *contrôleurs des manufactures* was confiscated and exhibited in public, together with the name of the maker and the merchant who purchased it. The defective article was then destroyed. If the fault were repeated, then both the maker and the merchant were themselves put on public display for a couple of hours, next to examples of their shoddy work.

However, these aggressive experiments in tight control of quality were gradually eclipsed, in the last years of Louis XIV's reign, by the King and Louvois' policy of war with Germany: the whole of France's economy turned away from domesticity and security – both of which encouraged the arts to flourish – towards military triumphs.

Louis XIV ignored the counsels of moderation and saving that Colbert pressed upon him, and the latter, in spite of his great achievements, his skill as a statesman and his contribution to the consolidation of the King's power, died in 1683 tired, rejected and saddened by the chaos that was spreading throughout France.

Charles Le Brun

The last, but by no means the least autocratic and despotic contributor to Louis XIV style, was the painter Charles Le Brun (1619–1690). His varied activities in many artistic fields – including painting and all forms of decorative art – were decisive in creating the style and taste which made France the leader and arbiter of fashion throughout Europe for two centuries, especially in interior decoration.

Le Brun's style, although praised and imitated by his contemporaries, does not excite great praise from critics of today. His talents were, in fact, chiefly those of a designer, as can be seen from the large works executed by him after his return from Rome, where he studied from 1642 to 1646 under Poussin. The frescoes in the *Galerie d'Hercule* and in the Hotel Lambert, as well as those for the Château de Vaux, which were commissioned by Fouquet, Superintendent of Finance, mark some of his early successes at Court. His painting of 1660 'The Generosity of Alexander', commissioned by Louis XIV, immediately earned him a prominent position at Court and marked the beginning of a career which lasted until the death of Colbert, who had originally recommended him to the King. The subsequent appointment as Director of the *Manufacture Royale des Meubles de la Couronne* incorporated with the *Manufacture Royale des Gobelins* gave Le Brun enormous effective power over all the palaces owned by the Crown, and he fulfilled his duty with great skill and a diligence that extended to the smallest details. He designed furniture, painted decorative panels, created motifs for the stucco cornices of the monumental ceilings, and prepared models and cartoons for tapestries, in every case achieving a faithful and flattering interpretation of the grandiose

ideas conceived by the King and approved by Colbert. Le Brun's sole aim was to provide the most magnificent possible background for the exploits of the Sun King and his splendid Court. The King entrusted him with the decoration of the Apollo Gallery at the Louvre, while at Versailles he executed the imposing decorations for the *Salon de Guerre*, the *Salon de Paix* and the *Galerie des Glaces*. This last is considered the finest achievement among all the sumptuous splendours of the Court of the *Grand Roi*.

Gobelins, Beauvais and Aubusson

Another important aspect of Le Brun's work was his direction and supervision of the immense organization of the *Manufacture des Meubles de la Couronne aux Gobelins*, in which carpenters, cabinet-makers, tapestry weavers, goldsmiths, engravers and chisellers were employed, and where tapestries were woven for the King. The work of the painter-director was of major importance in the history of the French tapestry industry; the whole production of the latter half of the seventeenth century shows his influence.

Le Brun designed models for magnificent tapestries inspired with the sole aim of glorifying the King. He kept minute and strict control of the quality of the products and was always very demanding and scrupulously careful in the choice of colours. With the collaboration of a regiment of artists trained in his school, Le Brun stimulated the *Manufacture*, continually stepping up production to meet the pressing and never-ending royal demands. The tapestries were often woven out of wool mixed with silk, the background being worked in gold or silver threads. The weaving was always done with a *haute lisse* (high warp).

The three series of tapestries depicting the Elements, the Seasons and 'The Little Gardeners' were woven to designs created by Le Brun, as was the series 'The History of the King', made between 1663 and 1670, illustrating highlights in the life of Louis XIV: his coronation, his victories, his wedding and so on. This series alone comprised 14 enormous tapestries, each $16\frac{1}{2} \times 23\frac{1}{2}$ feet, and was the most important work accomplished by the factory. Each episode was framed by a border of arabesque motifs, allegorical figures, weapons and trophies, all enhanced by interwoven gold threads.

'The Months' and 'Royal Palaces' two famous works, were also designed by Le Brun and put into cartoon form by a group of painters, among them Van der Meulen, who specialized in landscapes, and Monnoyer, who specialized in flowers. The months of the year were portrayed in symbolic form, each featuring a Royal palace, and were complemented by smaller tapestries called *entre-fenêtres*, on which the decorative motifs were repeated. Today this series is preserved in the Mobilier National in Paris. Finally, Le Brun's series 'The History of Alexander' must also be mentioned; the lavish flattery of the work now seems extravagant, but at the time it was highly praised and served to increase the reputation of the painter.

After the appointment of Louvois as Superintendent of the *Manufacture Royale*, and following the death of Colbert, Le Brun fell into obscurity and disgrace. He managed to keep his post as Director, but orders fell off and soon all but ceased. At his death in 1690 the painter Mignard, a protégé of Louvois, succeeded him, but by 1694 the continual wars and resulting financial crises necessitated the closure of the *Manufacture*. The Gobelins opened again in 1699, and the following year the painter Audran became Director. Louis XIV was still alive when Audran's series of tapestries known as 'Portals of the Gods' was made in 1709; the series called 'Twelve Months of Grotesques', also by Audran, was finished soon after. These tapestries illustrate a radical change in taste: inspired by the designs of Jean Berain, they are purely ornamental in character and contain the basic elements of the dominant style that was to be characteristic of the Louis XV period.

In 1664, on Colbert's advice, Louis XIV had granted the tapestry *Manufacture* at Beauvais the title of *Manufacture Royale des Tapisseries de Beauvais*, the difference being that the Gobelins produced tapestries exclusively for the King, while the tapestries at Beauvais were destined for the general market. Only towards the end of the century (1684), when the Fleming Pierre Behagle became Director, did Beauvais enjoy a period of creative activity. It was then that the masterpieces with motifs drawn from Berain's designs were woven, notably the 'Grotesques on a Yellow Ground', and also the magnificent set of four tapestries woven in wool silk and gold and silver thread, called the 'Naval Victories'. This last was commissioned by Madame de Montespan for her son the Comte de Toulouse, and shows great imagination and decorative flair.

The products of the *Manufactures* of Aubusson and Felletin cannot be compaired to those of the Gobelins and Beauvais; they specialized only in producing *verdures* – small tapestries worked with flowers, leaves and birds, all in various shades of green, interspersed with small ornamental figures or hunting scenes. Later, the *Manufacture* of Aubusson specialized in weaving *basse lisse* (low warp) tapestries and textiles for divans, chairs, firescreens and stools.

The palaces and royal châteaux

A special administration was required for the large number of Royal palaces, from the Louvre to Saint-Germain, from the Tuileries to Fontainebleau, from Saint-Cloud to Chambord, and of course Versailles, the building of which started in 1668. In 1663, with the King's approval, Colbert instituted the famous *Garde Meuble*. This had the clearly defined function of controlling and recording all the ordinances and payments, and the conservation of the furnishings in the Royal palaces. Another duty of the *Garde Meuble* was to keep an up-to-date Journal containing an inventory and description of every object acquired by the King. Each object was systematically numbered, and this enabled many pieces that might otherwise have been anonymous to be identified without difficulty at a later date.

The greatest cabinet-makers under Louis XIV were Domenico Cucci (died 1705) and André-Charles Boulle (1642–1732). Cucci, born in Todi, came to Paris in 1660, and worked for Cardinal Mazarin as a cabinet-maker and goldsmith. The cabinets made by this superlative artist are

Top: A console typifying the sumptuous, heavy style of Louis XIV furniture. Above left and right: Ornate Louis XIV guéridons, small tables on which lamps were placed

5

described in the *Garde Meuble* inventory as being fashioned *à la manière de Florence*, which means that they were inlaid with *commessi* (incrustation) in many types of semi-precious stones on black marble ground, and framed in ebony. Lapis lazuli, onyx and agate were all used, employing a technique developed in Florence under the patronage of the Grand Dukes of Tuscany, while the goldsmith Cucci added mounts and friezes in gilt bronze (ormolu), often using pewter in the inlay work for his cabinets, to enhance their polychrome effect. Many superb pieces of Cucci's work have been lost, including the two famous monumental cabinets called 'The Temple of Glory' and 'The Temple of Virtue' which had been displayed in the Galerie d'Apollo in the Louvre. Miraculously preserved and in good condition, however, are two other superb cabinets by the Italian *ébéniste* at Alnwick Castle, owned by the Duke of Northumberland. Of all furniture-makers of the time, however, André-Charles Boulle was the real innovator of the sumptuous, heavy style of furniture under Louis XIV and his name is closely linked to that style which characterizes the greatest era of French cabinet-making.

André-Charles Boulle, master cabinet-maker

André-Charles Boulle, cabinet-maker, was an even greater artist than Cucci. Recommended to Louis XIV by Colbert, Boulle at thirty had his own studio in the Louvre where he worked exclusively for the King. A characteristic feature of his pieces are the panels adorned with elaborate designs of arabesques and figures, which he made by super-imposing two pieces of equal thickness, one of tortoise-shell and one of metal, on which the decorative motif had been engraved. It was called either *première partie* or *contre partie*, depending on whether the background was composed of tortoiseshell or metal. In addition to the basic materials, bone ivory and mother-of-pearl might also be used to complete the inlay. The pieces were then decorated with mounts in gilt bronze, executed by Boulle himself, by Caffieri, or by other bronze founders. The only way of identifying a Boulle piece is by small details of style and despite the fact that many pieces are attributed to him, only a few can be said to be definitely his. Two chests or *commodes* in the Louvre, the payments for which are dated 1708–9 in the Journal, are without doubt his work, and the magnificent desk of the Elector of Bavaria, also in the Louvre, which dates from around 1715, can almost certainly be attributed to him. Boulle retired in 1715, but his four sons carried on his workshop.

As well as this master of the Louis XIV style, other contemporary cabinet-makers include Jean Macé, who lived and worked at the Louvre from 1664 to 1672, Pierre Gorle, Philippe Poitou, François Guillemart and Aubertin Gaudreau, all of whom employed similar techniques to those of Boulle. Generally, however, when the craze for chinoiserie came into fashion, they, along with makers like Martin Carlin and van Riesenberg, turned to producing pieces in this style. Unfortunately, though, few examples of this important aspect of Louis XIV style have survived, for judging from inventories, which mention many lacquered pieces, it was extremely popular.

Cabinet by Boulle, master cabinet-maker to Louis XIV

The Sun King's throne

Ceramics, carpets and silver also played a large part in interior decoration at the Court of Louis XIV. The extravagantly ornate silver, for example, was one of the marvels of Versailles, and Le Brun designed tables, seats and chairs all to be made out of solid, heavy silver. This provoked a response in the newspaper *Le Mercure Galant* to the effect that 'what was made of wood anywhere else, would, at Versailles, be made of silver'. The Sun King's throne, for instance, was eight feet high and was completely wrought in ornate silver. There were also many urns and dinner services all of embossed and chiselled silver.

Unfortunately such splendour was short-lived. In the financial crises caused by continual wars the silver objects were melted down to make coins, and none has survived. Faïence (glazed or enamelled earthenware) became a substitute for silver, and the motifs used are typified by those of the Royal tableware which were inspired by the drawings of Jean Berain (1640–1711). Berain was the innovator of a style based on symmetrical rectangles enclosing graceful designs of shells, scrolls bearing busts, and elongated vases, the clear beginnings of the *rocaille* style. The decorative motifs *à lambrequin* were also used; these were composed of close-knit flowering garlands surrounding vignettes of landscapes or chinoiserie scenes in blue on a white ground. The famous *style rayonnant*, much used on ceramics, was developed in the Rouen factories, and consisted of ornamental strapwork arranged, fan-like, around a central motif. The factories at Moustiers and Nevers used decorative motifs *en broderie* with light and delicate designs, imitating lace, on a white ground.

Carpets for the Royal residences were woven at Aubusson and Savonnerie. The workmanship was rather coarse, unlike that of oriental carpets, the weaving being done with a wool weft and hempen warp. Within the sumptuous borders were the same symbolic subjects as in the tapestries, all designed to enhance the glory of the King: thus the lion and the eagle symbolize courage and daring, and pomegranates and the fleur-de-lys are to be found in profusion. Thirteen carpets were commissioned by the King for the Galerie d'Apollo, about a hundred for the Royal apartments at the Louvre, and many others were placed in the throne room and in the *Grande Chambre du Roi* at the Tuileries. Forming part of the interior decoration, carpets complemented the themes of the architecture, the stucco friezes and the furnishings, and were at the same time designed to enrich and brighten the salons.

Towards the end of the seventeenth century many furnaces for the production of mirror glass were built; in 1665 Colbert was to institute the *Manufacture Royale des Glaces à Miroir* where, with the collaboration of glass-blowers under the direction of Noyen and the Italian, Perotti, who had emigrated to France from Altare, a new technique for casting mirror glass in sheets was developed. This meant that larger sheets of glass could be produced in France than in Venice, which had, until then, been the major centre for the manufacture of mirrors.

A new regime

The fifty-four long years of Louis XIV's reign were followed by a Regency of seven years. This the Sun King had entrusted before his death to Philippe d'Orléans, because his nephew, Louis, was still a minor. The regent, small and stocky with his curious gait, described as being like a carrier of water, and his rubicund face, his sight partially destroyed by a blow from a tennis racquet, was a man of considerable intelligence and breadth of mind. He was deeply interested in science and art, and his collection of paintings was judged the finest in Paris. He was not, however, a paragon of virtue. Dissolute in habit and a great gourmet, he delighted in giving intimate dinners at which riotous companions enjoyed his hospitality. They came to be known as the 'roués', and notorious scandals circulated in Paris about the immorality of the Court. Proof of his cynicism towards religious matters is provided by his reply to a letter from his daughter, the abbess of a convent at Chelles, who had signed herself 'bride of Christ' according to custom: 'I fear, dearest', he wrote, 'that I am on bad terms with my son-in-law'.

Philippe's first act as Regent was to abandon the splendour of Versailles, the sparkling maze of galleries and salons and the cold apartments with their monumental decorations. He banned irksome etiquette and the elaborate ceremonies and, to the delight of the Court, established himself in the magnificent Palais Royal, built by Richelieu. It became the scene of the Regent's parties and his affairs, both of which encouraged the cultivation of an attitude of dissolute elegance among the courtiers, in reaction to the boredom and monotony of the last ten years of Louis XIV's reign.

Looking at the interior decoration of this period, one has the impression that a fresh breeze swept away the oppressive formality of the old style. A lighter, somewhat affected style developed in its place, well suited to the taste of a society where elegance and luxury were the breath of life. Anything new was immediately popular; smaller, more intimate surroundings such as boudoirs and *petits appartements* became fashionable. Paler colours were used for interiors and furnishings; fabrics and *boiseries* were softened with graceful and delicate ornaments. The *rocaille* motif, for example, inspired by the elegant form of the *rocaille* (shell), was the highly successful creation of Juste-Aurèle Meissonnier (1693–1750), who developed and elaborated it in a vast series of drawings that were used by famous artists and skilled craftsmen: a graceful theme drawn from Nature was transformed and formalized until it assumed exquisitely intricate and sinuous shapes expressing every flight of fancy. In the hands of the expert goldsmiths and bronze workers, the *rocaille* motif began to appear on furniture, walls, fireplaces – now smaller in size – and around the large mirrors that reflected the light and enhanced the proportions of the salons.

The great cabinet-maker Charles Cressent, the Regent's favourite, softened the outlines of furniture with gilt bronze mounts composed of flowers, garlands and *singeries*, while female busts called *espagnolettes* adorned the corners of the *commodes* and harmonized with the exquisite marquetry worked in rare rosewood, purplewood and amaranth, creating the most beautiful colour combinations. The ornate historical tapestries disappeared – and with them the sombre hangings which darkened the walls – to be replaced by attractively coloured *boiseries* in pale yellow, apple green and delicate shades of lilac and ivory. The straight-backed chairs were replaced by soft bergères (a type of armchair). The *chaise longue*, devised for the *petit repos*, was also admirably suited to amorous conversations and court intrigues. The *causeuse*, a type of small sofa for two people, was introduced, and this too was much used for the exchange of scandalous gossip about the Regent's latest *béguins* (fancies). These themes developed and harmonized under Louis XV, and lasted until the middle of the century, slowly evolving into the gay and unbridled rococo style.

Louis XV, 'le roi bien-aimé'

Louis XV, to be described as one of the most loved and most hated of the kings of France, came to the throne when he was thirteen years old – that is, when he became of age. Startlingly handsome and gifted with a lively intelligence, he was orphaned when he was only three, proclaimed king at five, spoiled, praised and adored. Contrary to the assertions of his fiercest critics, Louis the *bien-aimé* spent much time and energy on the affairs of state at the beginning of his reign. In early adulthood, however, his attentions turned to women, and he became less interested in the affairs of state. The most important of his official mistresses was Madame de Pompadour, an intelligent, well-educated *bourgeoise* with considerable artistic talent, who dominates the history of France in this period both on account of her role in politics and above all her support of every form of artistic activity. Given the title *Maîtresse en titre du Roi,* Madame de Pompadour was officially presented at Court and allowed her own apartments at Versailles. She spent hours of her time and a lot of the King's money on art; she granted commissions and favours, and could number Voltaire, Rameau and Boucher among her admirers; Boucher was her personal portraitist, designer and confidant for sixteen years.

It was due to her efforts that the King became interested in the fortunes of the Royal porcelain factory at Sèvres, and increased its production. In addition to her other activities, Madame de Pompadour managed also to be the amusing and fascinating lover of a bored and lazy King who was happy to leave the affairs of state in the hands of his ministers and his favourite. He would go hunting or keep abreast of the many court intrigues, when he was not busying himself supervising the preparation of delicacies for intimate suppers in the *petits appartements* at Versailles or the Château de Choisy. Louis was completely indifferent to the philosophical and scientific debates of the time, and which found expression in the Encyclopedia on which Diderot and d'Alembert had worked with the collaboration of other intellectuals, notably Voltaire, Montesquieu and Turgot.

Louis XV furniture

Furniture occupies pride of place in the interior decoration of the Louis XV era. Its style, much imitated but never equalled, gained predominance in Europe as the result of the achievements of a relatively small group of *ébénistes* and *menuisiers* (carvers and joiners who did no inlay work

Above right: Rocaille (shell) motif on a candlestick design by Meissonnier. Below left: A simple Louis XV veilleuse or ottoman. Below right: A Louis XV bed à la turque

but specialized in the production of seat furniture and *console* tables superbly carved in the *rocaille* manner), of goldsmiths, tapestry weavers, engravers and sculptors. Small and charmingly named tables were devised for the convenience of the aristocracy: *poudreuses* for containing beauty patches and cosmetics; *coiffeuses* for hairpins and wigs; *guéridons*, supported on three slender legs with little castors, and round or oval tops edged with a tiny gallery in fretted brass, made to support the imaginatively wrought candlesticks. For more intimate use there were the *vide-poches* for men, tiny tables on which stood a dish designed to take the contents of a man's pockets when he emptied them before going to bed.

Among other delightful pieces were the graceful *tables de nuit*, equivalent to the modern bedside tables, and the dainty *bonheur-du-jour* (which was to be more popular in the following century), a small table surmounted by a miniature chest with tiny drawers around a central niche designed to take an inkstand and writing materials. There was also the *chiffonier*, round or oval in shape, with a top

A fine console that once belonged to Mme de Pompadour

usually made out of Sèvres porcelain, upon which gentlemen could put down their papers. For the intimate suppers the *servants*, small tables incorporating metal containers lined with felt, in which drinks could be kept cool, were introduced. The ingenious *table à la Tronchin* had a panel or flap adjusted by means of a sliding arm, and was useful for reading or drawing while standing. The most famous of this type of table was that designed by Migeon for the music room: it had six leaves and could accommodate a string sextet standing around it. Finally *secrétaires*, which appeared in 1730, were a type of cabinet with a high back, generally divided horizontally into two sections. The lower part was enclosed by a pair of doors, and had small drawers for private papers, while the top part carried niches and compartments closed by a flat top that could be lowered to provide a writing surface.

At the same time the desk or *bureau* was very popular in all its forms; these ranged from the *bureau plat* – simply a large table with two drawers in the frieze – to a top composed of little drawers and niches, often surmounted by a valuable gilt clock, rested on the writing surface. Another type was the *bureau en dos d'âne* or *bureau en tombeau*,

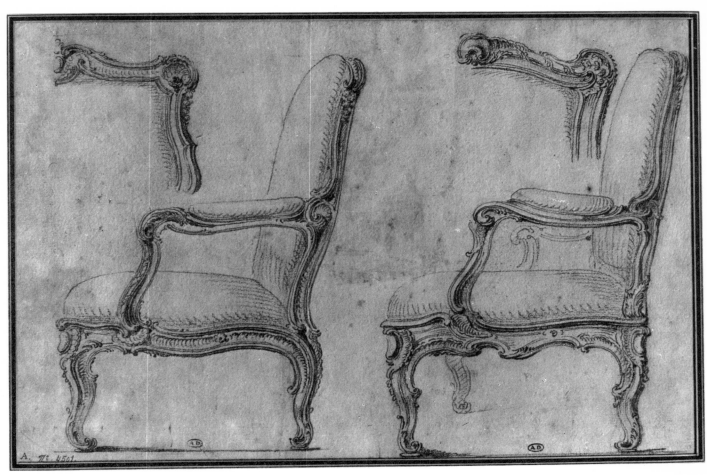

Chair designs from about 1735. A great variety of superbly carved chairs was invented in Louis XV's reign

their profiles resembling the back of a donkey or a sarcophagus respectively. The former had two flaps which could be pulled down from a central section, allowing two people to use it at the same time. A rare example of this type is the one made by the cabinet-maker Bernard van Riesenberg, probably for Louis XV's twin daughters, which is now in the Getty collection. The *bureau en pente*, with its sloping lid, has just one flap, while the *bureau à cylindre* differed from the others in that it had a semicircular lid that ran on grooves and receded into the back of the desk. The most perfect example of this type of bureau, said by many to be the most beautiful in the world, is the *bureau du Roi*, housed in Versailles. It was designed by Jean-François Oeben and made by an equally famous cabinet-maker, Jean-Henri Riesener, during the reign of Louis XVI.

An equally great variety of chairs was invented during Louis XV's reign. There were two main types: *meublant* and *courant*. *Meublant* chairs were designed to fill a purely decorative function and were ranged around the walls. Their decoration echoed the ornamental designs of the *boiseries* (wooden panelling covering the walls), and the stucco work. The other type, *courant*, was arranged in the centre of salons and drawing rooms and around tables; their backs were more elaborate than those of the *meublant*, but they were relatively light in weight and could be moved easily.

One of the most common chairs of the age was the *bergère*, a large and comfortable chair, in which the upholstery of the back continued round to cover the arms in a simple curving shape. As a rule, it had a finely carved wooden frame, and was often painted and gilded as well. The *bergère* was often covered in silk, tapestry or *petit point*. If the back let down for greater comfort, then it was known as a *bergère en commodité*, while another variation was the *bergère en confessional*, which had low recessed arms and two wings attached to the back to provide a comfortable head-rest. The small divan made for two, often called a *tête-à-tête*, was also referred to as a *marquise, confidante* or *causeuse*. Complete relaxation was provided by the *chaise longue*, a type of *bergère* with an elongated seat on which to rest one's legs. When divided into two detachable parts it was known as the *chaise longue brisée*, a modified version of the *chaise longue à la duchesse*, which, as well as supporting the legs, provided a foot-rest in the form of a low rail.

In the vast *salons* people had to keep close to the fire-places, and the *chauffeuse* was devised for this purpose. It had a low seat, short legs and a rounded back to shelter the uncovered shoulders of the ladies. The *coiffeuse*, with its low arms, was designed to accompany the little toilet tables. It had a curved back to allow greater manoeuvrability for the creators of the ladies' elaborate hair-styles. Finally, a typical example of the ideal of comfort at all costs was the *voyeuse*, a chair designed for the person who simply wanted to watch a card game, but not take part in it,

10

and which enabled him to lean comfortably against a stuffed cushion set into the chair back.

Above all, however, the *commode* or chest remains the most typical piece of Louis XV furniture. Following the more majestic *commodes* of Louis XIV and the Regency, the Louis XV *commode* reflects the new style in the absence of ponderous ornamentation. The number of drawers was reduced to two, the sides became rounded, and the structural line softened into gentle curves. Lively decoration was provided by polychrome marquetry of grapes and flowers and gilt bronze mounts which adorned each piece with a riot of curved branches, scrolls and symbolic masks, the work of such masters of sculpture in bronze as Cressent, Caffieri, the Slodtz brothers and many others. Doors replace drawers in the *commodes à vantaux* whose panels were inlaid with marquetry of baskets of flowers and fruit or decorated with chinoiserie scenes in lacquer-work.

The downfall of the rocaille

Furniture enriched with gilt mounts and brilliant with brightly coloured marquetry, fanciful and elegant in form, rapidly became fashionable, and reached its highest point of taste and fashion by the middle of the eighteenth century. It was however modified during the second half of the century, when artists' attentions were attracted to the monuments of the classical age, which were discovered as a result of excavations in Italy (Herculaneum in 1738, Pompeii in 1749). First-century paintings and interior decoration were brought to light in these works, along with a large number of decorative household objects, which together provided important clues as to the classical style.

These discoveries encouraged a less frivolous taste and greater formal balance in composition and decoration. Madame de Pompadour became a champion of a new, more sober fashion (known as neoclassicism), under the influence of the engraver Cochin, who was a relentless critic of the excesses of the *rocaille* style.

An important sequel to the admonitions of Cochin and the influence of the Italian archaeological discoveries was J. Winkelman's 'History of Art and Antiquity', published in 1764, in which the German scholar stated his view that artists must produce serious and lasting work, inspired solely by classical art. The book was widely read and respected, and slowly the design of furniture and of interior decoration in general became more restrained. Detail in the classical style replaced the scrolls and turns of the *rocaille*; acanthus leaves and beading now decorated furniture of more rigidly architectonic design. The Louis XVI style was beginning to emerge, fourteen years before the accession of the King who gave it its name.

The royal porcelain

One of Madame de Pompadour's most outstanding achievements was to interest Louis XV in the ceramic arts. Thanks to her, Royal protection was granted to the factory at Vincennes which was to become the *Manufacture Royale des Porcelaines de France*, and on her advice it was moved in 1756 from Vincennes to Sèvres, becoming the King's own

A bergère, extremely popular in the reign of Louis XVI

property in 1760. With such illustrious patronage and with a team of painters, modellers and sculptors who were all experts in their own field, the *Manufacture de Sèvres* had a meteoric success, becoming even more fashionable in Europe than Meissen. At the Royal banquets, Sèvres dinner services, coffee sets and jugs appeared; Arcadian themes, inspired by the paintings of Boucher, Watteau and Fragonard, were copied in miniature and painted in reserved panels against the famous *bleu du Roi* or the enchanting *rose Pompadour* backgrounds. The flower was the dominant decorative theme, developed in a naturalistic style: single flowers and flowers in bunches were mingled together on plates and cups; twisted flowering branches formed the handles to the cups, teapots and vases; delicate leaves became spouts and knobs. The magnificent *bleu du Roi* was sometimes complemented by medallions, framed by delicate garlands of wild flowers and roses, and later by the partridge-eye motif (a series of small dots on a coloured background).

Tapestries were no longer heavy and pompous, but were made smaller and with more light-hearted subjects than in the reign of the Sun King. The painter Oudry was Director of the Gobelins for many years, and as a result of his efforts tapestries started to imitate painting and become purely ornamental in function. This trend increased when Boucher directed the factory and designed cartoons featuring pastoral scenes and rustic idylls. Some good examples are his 'Loves of the Gods', 'The Story of Psyche', and 'The Italian Feast Day' series, all woven in the popular *seconde teinture chinoise*. Typical of this style are the 'alentours' tapestries in which the composition, enclosed by a characteristic frieze of twisted climbing plants, stands out against a background that resembles a wall draped with Damascus silk. The decorations· around the frieze are composed of cascades of fruit, garlands, putti, monkeys, trophies and cornucopias. Charles Coypel designed the 'Story of Don Quixote', woven in twenty-eight pieces, 'Extracts from the Opera', and 'Scenes from the Opera', all in the alentour style.

Throughout the century, there was a strong interest in chinoiserie and in exotica in general, which had started in the previous reign. This is seen in Desportes' series 'New Indies', in Perronneau's picturesque 'Turkish Massage', and in A. van Loo's 'Turkish Scene'. Mythology and gallantry, other themes of the age, are evident in the work of De Troyes, notably the 'Daphnis and Chloë' series, 'The Loves of the Gods' and 'The Story of Esther'. Prestige tapestry appears again in 'Louis XV's Hunts', designed by Oudry. This is a series of nine pieces woven between 1739 and 1745, in which the luxuriant forests of Compiègne and Fontainebleau provide a green and leafy background for those taking part in the King's hunt. It was Oudry who assured the fortunes of the tapestry industry at Beauvais when he became Director in 1734. With Nicolas Besnier he did the cartoons for the 'Comedies of Molière', 'Rustic Pleasures', and Huet's 'Pastoral Scenes'. Between 1773 and 1779 a series of eight tapestries was woven from cartoons by Casanova entitled 'Country Pleasures'. This was the last important work produced at Beauvais, and subsequently the factory specialized in weaving tapestries to cover sofas and chairs.

Like his great predecessor, Louis XV did not hesitate in moments of financial crisis to replenish the State coffers by melting down his and his subjects' silver; more pieces were to disappear during the Revolution, and as a result very few have survived to this day. Among the most important goldsmiths were the artist Meissonnier, the designer Thomas Germain, the Slodtz brothers and Oppenordt. The latter were notable creators of beautiful vessels for the dinner table and for coffee drinking, sinuous in line and with fanciful fluted work and spirals. The *écuelle* is a typical piece in this style; it is a large shallow cup, embellished with engraved or chased ornament, with vegetable or floral details rendered with a remarkable degree of realism on its cover. Alongside the *écuelle* there was the *taste-vin*, decorated with designs inspired by grapes and vines. Unfortunately no trace remains of the famous gold *torchères* wrought for the King by the great Germain, but examples of the *surtouts* or *épergnes* depicting hunting or other subjects are still to be seen. These are small masterpieces of sculpture, made to occupy a position of honour in the centre of the King's lavish table. Jacques Caffieri wrought magnificent gilt bronzes of this nature; some of his finest work adorned the Passement clock. He also made andirons in elegant shapes and decorated fireplaces, furniture and clocks with elaborate work in the charming *rocaille* style. Finally, our description would be incomplete without a mention of the sixteen original statuettes in gilded silver, representing the countries of the world and cast by Cousinet for the King of Portugal and of the splendid *épergne* portraying a deer hunt wrought by Jacques Roettier, one of the more restrained and discerning masters of the *rocaille* style, for the Elector of Cologne.

Louis XVI: 'too young to reign'

A twenty-year old King, shy and insecure, and his Queen of only eighteen – Marie-Antoinette, daughter of the Empress Maria Teresa – came to the throne and ruled for eighteen years, until the tragic upheaval of the Revolution spelt the end of the *Ancien Régime*, during which France had dazzled Europe with the richness of her decorative art, her culture, her thinkers and her enlightened philosophers. The cry of the young couple on the death of Louis XV was prophetic: 'What a disaster, we are too young to reign!'

Louis XVI, referred to as 'that poor chap' by his inconsiderate young wife, was fat and greedy, often eating four cutlets, a *poule grasse*, six eggs and a large plate of ham at one sitting, and then working off the fat with exercises and hunting. Most of all he liked trying his hand at various crafts, and his first thought on coming to the throne was to instal a carpenter's shop in part of his predecessor's apartments, along with a goldsmith's and a blacksmith's shop. There, with his trusted Germain, he busily worked at his forge and made locks, padlocks and strong boxes in iron. Although endowed with common sense, Louis XVI was completely unprepared for the art of government, for until his accession no one had thought of explaining it to him. The responsibilities which fell to his lot weighed heavily on his mind, a mind weak and indecisive in character and full of complexes. He was oppressed by the thought that 'each of his laws would decide the fate of his twenty-five million subjects'. The result was that he gave way to the judgments of his ministers and ultimately to that of his wife.

The young King was as hesitant and shy as the youthful Marie-Antoinette was vivacious and spontaneous. She adored frivolous novelties, jewels, elegance and laughter, but could not boast much education. A letter from her mother suggests how immature she was; it warns her 'Do not endanger the reputation that you have acquired, which has come neither from your gifts nor your intelligence, for both, as you know, are limited . . .'

A change in style

Furniture continued to dominate interior decoration during the reign of Louis XVI. As has already been mentioned, the curved line became less popular, bringing about a gradual simplification of design between 1760 and 1765 that illustrated the influence of the discoveries from the archaeological sites at Herculaneum. The murals which were uncovered there, with their decorative style and portrayal of everyday household objects, awakened a passionate interest in everything reminiscent of the classical age, especially in the field of interior decoration. When this new style favoured by Madame de Pompadour began to develop, a slight alteration in structural line was apparent. In Louis XVI's reign, the change became more marked. Furniture became more compact as the taste for sophisticated prettiness waned; the classical style, subjective in inspiration, was adopted in reaction against the fantastical caprice of the Louis XV style.

Gilt bronze was still used to decorate furniture in the

reign of Louis XVI; only the designs had changed. The most common themes were those drawn from the classical decorative repertoire – notably fluting, friezes and garlands – while chairs were given rounded backs, of medallion or oval shape. The passion for chinoiserie and lacquered furniture lasted for a short period with the additional use of a varnish resembling Chinese lacquer, called *vernis Martin* after the Martin brothers, who invented it. Medallions in plaster and Sèvres porcelain adorned the *bonheurs-du-jour*, the *toilettes* and the *encoignures*. The technique of marquetry was perfected as cabinet-makers enjoyed a greater choice of precious woods; at least fifty were available by that time, many of them soft and delicate in tone. Designs became geometric in inspiration, the woods being arranged in beautifully coloured strips which created glowing patterns. Lozenge shapes enclosing delicate flower or leaf motifs were the speciality of Jean-Henri Riesener, the greatest cabinet-maker of this period.

About 1775, in place of marquetry composed of many different woods and stains, cabinet-makers began to use mahogany. This hard, solid, fine wood, russet in colour and with attractive figuring (the natural pattern in the grain of the wood), satisfied the taste for greater simplicity. Furniture was made in the Etruscan style, using all the ornamental quality of mahogany. The essential components of this style were simple straight lines; the strictly classical proportions were enhanced by sober bronze ornamentation derived from the classical friezes. Unfortunately, no example of this style has survived, although it is known that the artist David designed many pieces for his sumptuous home.

Unlike Madame de Pompadour, Marie-Antoinette did not make any significant contribution to the current style, but merely displayed a lively interest in anything exotic. An example of her taste can be seen in the creation of a *boudoir à la turque* at Fontainebleau, where two perfume-burners and pillars surmounted by busts of odalisks lend the correct exotic air. During her reign, the Queen refurnished her private apartments at Versailles, Compiègne and Fontainebleau, using the services of a group of foreign, principally German, cabinet-makers whom she summoned to France.

Jean-Henri Riesener, the greatest cabinet-maker in the Louis XVI style, was German in origin but worked from an early age in Oeben's studio. Georges Jacob, one of the most gifted *menuisiers* of his time, C. Charles Saunier and Jean Leleu are among the most famous of the little group of French cabinet-makers at Court; Nicolas Petit, and René Dubois were also important. These were some of the principal craftsmen of the Louis XVI era, and to their names can be added those of the Germans summoned to Paris by the Queen: Adam Weisweiler, David Roentgen (a particular favourite of Marie-Antoinette), Bernard Molitor, Wilhelm Benneman and J. Stockel.

The descriptive terms for Louis XVI furniture do not change much from those used under Louis XV. The *commode*, or chest, continued to be fashionable, and the *commode à encoignure* was developed. It had a corner cupboard at each end, forming one large piece. Stockel, the cabinet-maker, invented an imposing *commode en croissant*. Some *commodes* were made as large as ten feet, while others, termed *demi-commodes*, were smaller. The *bureau-plat* remained a favourite, its legs now embellished with bronze feet and fluted mouldings. The *cabinet* was popular, for example, in the form of the *meuble à bijoux*, where ladies could keep their jewels. Cabinet-makers continued to produce the *bureau à cylindre*. The famous *bureau du Roi* started by Oeben, was finished by Riesener during this period. Other old favourites remained popular: tables *à la Tronchin*, *chiffoniers*, *guéridons*, *vide-poches*, and the *servants*. Marie-Antoinette's passion for gambling encouraged the building of occasional tables and card tables of all types, and the *voyeuse* chairs for the comfort of spectators of the game were more in demand than ever.

Beds, chairs and silks

The most popular bed was that *à l'Artois*, with its ornate baldaquin fixed to the wall, closely followed by those *à la polonnaise*. The *duchesse* bed continued to play its part in the sovereign's *grands levers* and *petits levers*. It too had a baldaquin fixed to the wall, and short hangings that allowed an uninterrupted view of the occupant of the bed. Beds placed longways against the wall, *à la turque*, became fashionable in the second half of the century. Chairs kept the names they were given in the previous century. One of the most gifted *menuisiers* in the Louis XVI style was Georges Jacob, who simplified the complex profile of chairs and seats by introducing oval or round backs with frames lightly carved to resemble creepers, or else lyre backs and even balloon-shaped backs, in honour of the Montgolfier brothers who launched the first hot-air balloon in 1783. Jacob developed the Etruscan chair and divans to seat several people, and also the upholstered sofa, with a large number of legs and rigid arms bearing delicate inlays in the form of animals.

Little or no attention was paid to the tapestry industries at Gobelins and Beauvais, which merely continued to produce the type of hangings that were popular in the previous century; the new designs are not worth noting. The possibilities of the pictorial style introduced by Oudry were explored, and although they were still called 'tapestries' they were in fact little scenes woven in silk and wool, copying the paintings of Greuze and van Loo. Portraits of courtiers were also produced; framed like pictures, they were often hung next to the original paintings. Series like the 'Costumes and Manners of the Levant' were woven from van Loo's designs; Callot's 'The Seasons' clearly shows classical influence, with a profusion of altars, tripods, columns, Roman feasts and figures clad in togas. In a vaguer, less well-defined fashion, these same themes are used for filling-in purposes in the cycle 'The History of France', and in the series entitled 'The Assassination of Coligny' and the 'Death of Leonardo da Vinci'.

It was the Lyons silk industry rather than the tapestry industry which expanded during Marie-Antoinette's reign, and silk became an indispensable furnishing fabric. Under the eye of Philippe Lasalle, working at Lyons, silk weaving attained technical perfection, achieving a refined decorative elegance by the shading of colours and tones in order to capture the effects of light and shade, exploiting the qualities of contrast and shading in a new and original way. Lasalle created imaginative compositions using floral themes, bouquets interwoven with fluttering ribbons,

draperies, garlands and symbolic figures. The finest
example of his work is the fabric woven for Catherine the
Great which symbolizes the triumph of the Russian eagle by
standards placed above a trophy of Turkish arms. Other
artists who excelled in silk were Jean Pillement and
Gaspard Grégoire, the gifted craftsmen who produced
splendid figured velvets at Lyons. Among the many types of
silk produced at Lyons is a type of taffeta called *chiné à la
branche* (watered silk) which bears a resemblance to the
famous *pointe de Hongrie* embroidery. Lyons silks were
used to produce many splendid masterpieces, but around
1760 in Jouy, a village near Versailles, a German called
Oberkampf (1738–1815) began producing painted linens
with designs taken from the painter Jean-Baptiste Huet.
They were done in delicate colour on a natural or light
background, using themes inspired by Chinese art or copied
from Indian materials. Oberkampf also exploited the contemporary vogue in literature by printing episodes from the
successful novel 'Paul et Virginie' by Bernadin de Saint-
Pierre. Later, embracing the classical style, linens were
produced at Jouy in large tinted strips enlivened by tiny
wreaths, little *scènes à la grecque*, and mythological subjects.

All the works made there became highly sought-after, and
Louis XVI eventually conferred the title *Manufacture
Royale* on the factory.

Papiers-peints

Papier-peint (painted wallpaper) was an important
innovation in the field of wall decoration. It required an
even-textured paper on which decorative motifs and
pictorial compositions were painted, and soon became
popular as it was less costly than silks and brocades, as
well as being more colourful and varied in composition. It
was the elegant forerunner of modern machine-printed
wallpaper.

Papier-peint had already enjoyed a short period of
popularity when examples of paintings were imported from
China, usually featuring bamboo plants, birds and peach
blossom. Designs influenced by these paintings became
fashionable in France at the end of the eighteenth century,
and the fashion spread throughout Europe, where wallpaper was known as *carte de France*. The most successful
manufacturer of papiers-peints was J-B. Reveillon who, in
1763, collaborated with such decorative painters as Pillement, Lavalle, Poussin, the younger Boucher, and Huet to
found the most famous factory in France. From 1763 to
1771, Reveillon, expressing the taste of the moment,
reproduced popular themes from the classical world and
also incorporated themes inspired by Nature: trees, flowers
and birds appeared on all his papers. *Papiers-peints* were
also used on screens and firescreens, and in 1783 the Montgolfier brothers used them in the construction of their
balloon.

The classical style was slow to influence the production
of the *Manufacture de Sèvres*. Only around 1774 did the
caprice and fantasy typical of the rococo style give way to
more restrained designs. Cups, teapots and coffeepots
became cylindrical or barely curved in shape, the handles
no longer made in the form of flowering shoots but in
plain rectangles instead, and their edges decorated with
borders of Greek key pattern or classical palmettes; urns

A Louis XVI guéridon. After going out of fashion under
Louis XV, such tables regained popularity under Louis XVI

and small sphinxes acted as knobs on lids, and sometimes
served as handles. Gold was more widely used than before,
both as a background colour and also to complement the
popular motifs of dainty garlands of rosettes with delicate
branches. Gold encircled the medallions bearing the pur-
chaser's monogram placed in a prominent position in the
centre of each piece, on a white or ivory ground. Typical of
the later period, especially from 1781–4 is the 'jewel'
decoration, invented by Coteau: drops of coloured enamel
in relief were set like jewels in gold work, also in relief. In
the field of 'biscuit' porcelain, arcadian and gallant subjects
gave way to mythological ones; it was to the skill of Etienne
Falconet, the brilliant modeller of exquisite figures, that
France owed her leadership in this field. From this period
dates the famous dinner service commissioned by Catherine
the Great, which is held to be the most beautiful produced
during the whole era. Completed in 1779, it comprised
about 800 pieces, decorated in medallions of Pompeian
red with designs inspired by antique cameos, intercon-
nected with gilded branches. The decoration is set against a
superb background of light blue, and each piece bears a
monogram surmounted by the Imperial crown.

During the reign of Louis XVI there was continuous
activity in the Savonnerie carpet *Manufacture*. At first the
decorative motifs used during the Louis XV period were
retained, in an enlarged and elaborated form, but these
were eventually replaced by the classical style. The carpets
were enclosed by a wide border of classical Greek design,
and some popular themes were inspired by Italian archaeological finds: Roman helmets, trophies, chariots and temple
ruins. Marie-Antoinette's taste for the exotic found expression in this field also to the standard designs. However, the
production from the Savonnerie was seriously reduced by
the end of the century.

A great many bronze workers were employed in the
production of *appliques*, mounts for vases of semi-precious
stone, furniture, mirrors and clocks. The greatest of these
was without doubt Pierre Gouthière (1732–1813). Between
1772 and 1777 he wrought all the bronze at Fontainebleau,
which was being renovated by the architect Gabriel by the
order of Marie-Antoinette. He worked for the Duchesse de
Mazarin and, at Louvecienne, on Madame du Barry's
pavilion. His marvellous gilt bronze mounts complemented

the Duc d'Aumont's passion for urns, objets d'art, and semi-precious gems, of which he had a large collection. An exceptionally fine example is the beautiful serpentine urn surmounted by splendid female figures wrought in bronze, which belonged to Marie-Antoinette and is now to be seen in the Louvre. Gouthière also decorated the magnificent red jasper perfume-burner, carved in the shape of a fluted vase and set on a tripod in the form of goat's feet. This is preserved in the Wallace Collection in London, along with another Gouthière piece, the Avignon clock, made after a design by Boizot. Both are signed and dated.

An eminent contemporary of Gouthière was Philippe Caffieri II, son of Jacques, Louis XV's great *fondeur-ciseleur* (caster and chaser). Caffieri collaborated with his father in making the famous Passement astronomical clock (*Cabinet de la Pendule*, Versailles) and he wrought a candelabrum for Bayeux Cathedral. More important however, because of the classical influence that it displays, is his Easter candelabrum in Clermont-Ferrand Cathedral, which is made in the form of a tripod with goat's hooves, decorated with interlaced garlands and looped ribbons.

Among the greatest exponents of the Louis XVI style were R. J. Auguste and J. N. Roettier. Auguste, who worked at a number of European courts, was among the first to embrace the new classical style; his designs were as simple as possible, both for objets d'art and for pictorial compositions, and they closely resembled genuine antique pieces. Notable among his works are the elegant classical candelabrum wrought for the King of Sweden, Louis XVI's coronation crown, on which he worked with the goldsmith Aubert. J. Nicholas Roettier, trained by his father, was employed on the monumental dinner service that Catherine the Great commissioned for her favourite, Count Orloff, between 1770 and 1771. The rare technical skill and the perfect modelling and casting of the form and decoration featuring an exquisite ivy garland, made this service a masterpiece of its time. The greater part remains in Russia but a few pieces are preserved in the Musée Nissim de Camondo in Paris. François-Thomas Germain was active during this period; he was the son of the great Thomas from whom he inherited a famous and well-established shop and the most illustrious clientèle in Europe. But his activities ended with a disastrous bankruptcy in 1765, for he had remained faithful to the paternal rules and regulations from which he never managed to free himself. He had not progressed beyond the outmoded rococo style.

Whoever the workman, however, the principal characteristic of the Louis styles, that of a certain instinctive elegance, remains constant and without parallel; even today, when a sumptuous interior is commissioned, the designer often turns to eighteenth-century France for inspiration. In these pages we have seen the evolution of styles during three great reigns – the change from oppressive formality under Louis XIV to the free elaboration and – later – more rhythmic simplicity of Louis XV and Louis XVI. The palace which witnessed the rise and fall of three monarchs, Versailles, was stripped of much of its contents during the Revolution, but remains as unsurpassed evidence of the Grand Style that influenced the whole of Europe in its day. This was indeed a unique phase in the history of decorative art – a phase that ended when Louis XVI and Marie-Antoinette left Versailles for the last time.

Index of artists

Aubert, Jean 15
Audran, Gérard 5
Auguste, Robert Joseph 15, 61
Avril, Etienne 57
Baumhauer, Joseph 31
Behagle, Pierre 5
Benneman, Wilhelm 13, 47
Berain, Jean 5, 6, 21
Berain, Jean II 21
Besnier, Nicolas 12
Boizot, Louis Simon 15, 62, 63
Bouchardon 25
Boucher, François 8, 11, 14, 25
Boulle, André-Charles 5, 6, 17, 19, 20, 29, 31, 40
Caffieri, Jacques 6, 11, 12, 15, 23, 25, 31, 43
Caffieri, Philippe II 15
Callot, Jacques 13
Carlin, Martin 6, 49, 53, 54
Casanova 12
Cochin, Charles Nicolas 11
Commelin 54
Coteau 14
Cousinet 12
Coypel, Charles 12
Cressent, Charles 7, 11, 23, 25, 40
Cresson, Jean-Baptiste 37
Cucci, Domenico 5, 6
Dauthiau 25
Dégault 58
Delorme, Jean-Louis Faizelot 31
Delunes, N. P. 60
Desmalter, Jacob 29
Desportes, François 12
De Troyes, Jean-François 12
Dubois, René 13, 51
Duplessis 27
Du Tertre 60
Duvivier, Claude 43
Falconet, Etienne 14
Falconet, Louis 64
Falconet, Maurice 51
Fortier, Alexandre 31, 47
Fragonard, Jean Honoré 11
Gabriel, Jacques-Ange 14, 47
Gallé 29
Garnier, Pierre 35
Gaudreau, Antoine 33
Gaudreau, Aubertin 6, 23
Gerbu, Gabriel 61
Germain, François-Thomas 12, 15
Germain, Pierre 12, 43
Germain, Thomas 12, 15, 43
Girard, François 39
Gorle, Pierre 6
Gouthière, Pierre Joseph 14, 15, 48, 60, 62
Grégoire, Gaspard 14
Greuze, Jean-Baptiste 13
Guillemart, François 6
Hervieu 27
Huet, Jean-Baptiste 12, 14
Jacob, Georges 13, 64
Joubert, G. 33
La Croix, Roger (Vandercreuse) 37, 38
Lasalle, Philippe 13

Lavalle 14
Le Brun, Charles 3, 4, 6
Lelarge, Jean-Baptiste 58
Leleu, Jean-François 13, 49, 53, 55
Lepine 27
Le Riche 63
Le Roy, Julien 52
Levasseur, Etienne 29
Macé, Jean 6, 17
Manger, Jean 19
Marchand, Nicolas Jean 31
Martin brothers 13, 35
Meissonnier, Juste-Aurèle 7, 21, 43
Menière, F. N. 63
Michel, Claude (Clodion) 48
Migeon, Pierre 9
Migeon, Pierre II 36
Mignard, Pierre 5
Molitor, Bernard 13
Monnoyer, Jean-Baptiste 4
Nogaret, Pierre 39
Noyen 7
Oberkampf 14
Oeben, Jean François 10, 13, 27, 37, 49, 54, 55, 56
Oppenordt, Gilles-Marie 12
Oudry, Jean-Baptiste 11, 12, 13
Payrotte, Alexandre 29
Peronneau, Jean-Baptiste 12
Perotti 7
Petit, Nicolas 13
Pierre, Jean-Baptiste 29
Pillement 14
Pineau, Nicolas 23
Poirier 47
Poitou, Philippe 6
Poussin, Nicolas 4, 14
Reizell, F. 33
Réveillon, J. 14
Riesener, Jean-Henri 10, 13, 27, 33, 37, 45, 48, 50, 56
Roentgen, David 13, 47
Roettier, Jacques-Nicolas 12, 61
Roettier, Jean-Nicolas 15
Roumier, Claude 35
Rousseau, Antoine 47
Rousseau brothers 45, 47
Saunier, Claude Charles 13, 52, 56
Schwerdferger, Jean Ferdinand 58
Slodtz brothers 11, 12, 23, 33
Stockel, Joseph 13, 47
Stollewerck, Michel 31
Thomire 58
Tilliard, Jean-Baptiste 39
Tilliard, Jean-Baptiste II 39
Topino, Charles 36
Van Clève 47
Van der Meulen, Adam Frans 4
Van Loo, A. 12, 13
Van Loo, Claude 13, 29
Van Riesenberg, Bernard 6, 10
Verbeckt, Jacques 25, 41
Vitel 51
Watteau, Antoine 11
Weisweiler, Adam 13, 49, 55
Winkelman, J. 11

1   André-Charles Boulle (1642–1732). Ebony *commode*. Versailles.

This *commode*, decorated with marquetry of ebony and brass, and mounted with winged sphinxes of gilt bronze, was made by Boulle about 1708–9 for Louis XIV's apartments in Versailles. André-Charles Boulle, born in Paris on 11 November 1642, the son of a joiner, was to become one of the most famous French cabinet-makers under Louis XIV. It is said that he was related to Pierre Boulle, a Swiss cabinet-maker who worked for Louis XIII. Boulle was highly talented; documents of the time describe him variously as a painter, architect, engraver, sculptor in bronze, and *marqueteur*. His skill as a painter won him nomination to the Accademia di San Luca.

On the death of the cabinet-maker Jean Macé, Colbert recommended Boulle to the Sun King and on 22 May 1672 procured for him the appointment as successor to Macé with the right to use a workshop in the Louvre, a privilege which enabled the artist to evade the law forbidding cabinet-makers from working in metal.

Boulle worked solely to provide furniture for the decoration of the Royal palaces, especially Versailles. One of his most important achievements was the splendid decoration in the Dauphin's *Grand Cabinet* situated on the first floor of the Palace of Versailles. The work was begun in 1681 and completed in 1683. One year later it was decided to move every piece to the ground floor of the Palace where, in the course of a few years, it was all destroyed by damp. The *commode* illustrated here is preserved with a matching one, in the Palace of Versailles.

2   A detail of one of the bronze sculptures that adorn the *commode*. Boulle himself wrought the bronze decorations.

4

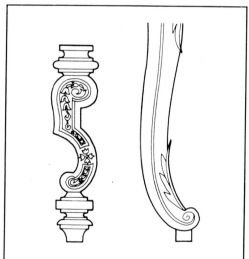

5

3 André-Charles Boulle (?) Imposing cabinet with two figures. Wallace Collection, London.

Experts disagree about the authorship of this piece, although the upper part with its fine marquetry work is definitely attributed to André-Charles Boulle.

The whole piece is inlaid with purplewood, tortoiseshell, pewter and brass set in an ebony veneer. It consists of an upper part with six drawers on either side of a door, surmounted by a central drawer bearing a gilt bronze portrait medallion of Louis XIV, surrounded by a laurel wreath. The top drawers on either side are smaller and have the fleur-de-lys of France inlaid in pewter and brass. The remaining drawers are decorated with floral marquetry and ebony veneer, each with a gilt bronze keyhole escutcheon in the centre. The sides of the cabinet are inlaid with flowers and vine trails.

The caryatid-style figures which support the upper part of the cabinet represent Summer and Autumn and were probably added at a later date. The back part of the lower half is veneered with purplewood, enclosing three marquetry panels of flowering branches within delicate pewter borders. The medallion bearing the bust of the Sun King is the work of Jean Manger (1648–1722).

4 *Veilleuse* or *lit de repos*.

This type of divan with a double back was very fashionable under Louis XIV, and later became popular when it was divided into three parts and called the *duchesse brisée*. The example shown here, also described as a *méridienne*, is in cane-work with a wooden frame carved in floral designs, and is supported on eight legs ending in scroll feet. This type of divan was usually completed with soft cushions.

5 Drawing of legs in the Louis XIV style.

The two types shown are: a leg with a double curve, inlaid shaft and peg-top foot; and a cabriole leg, simple in line, with a delicate acanthus leaf carving.

6, 7   The Thurel Clock. Conservatoire des Arts et Métiers, Paris.

This most beautiful example of the cabinet-maker's art is composed of a pedestal bearing the famous spherical clock, supported by bronze figures. Experts disagree about the attribution of the lower half to Boulle – indeed many of the attributions to the great cabinet-maker are based on details of style alone, and are open to doubt, for Boulle never signed his work, as the laws that obliged cabinet-makers to do so were introduced after the artist's death. His many sons continued to work in his style, especially André, later known as Boulle de Sèvres.

6

7

8

8 Plate of Rouen faience with the *rayonnant* design.

The circle radiating from a central motif or wheel pattern is a typical example of Rouen faience of the end of the seventeenth century and the beginning of the eighteenth. The 'Berain' decorative style, so called after the artist who inspired it, was highly fashionable at that time. Berain's designs were also exploited at the faience factories at Marseilles and Moustier.

9, 10 Juste-Aurèle Meissonnier (Turin 1693–Paris 1750). Two candlesticks in the rococo style in gilt and chased bronze. Wallace Collection, London.

The candlesticks have a pair of Cupids entwined around the stem. At the base of each is a stamp of the letter C surmounted by a crown, showing that tax had been paid on them. They were made after a design by Meissonnier, who was a decorator, painter, goldsmith and sculptor of Italian origin, he worked in Paris where he was appointed to the office of Royal goldsmith and designer to the *Cabinet du Roi*. He took over the latter office in 1726, in succession to Jean Berain II. Meissonnier did many designs for furniture, bronzes and ornamentations, which helped to spread the rococo style in France. The artist was also summoned to the Spanish and Portuguese courts, and in 1735 he designed a famous dinner service for the second Duke of Kingston.

Little, however, remains today to illustrate the artist's great activity, apart from a series of albums containing over a hundred decorative designs of various types.

9

10

11

12

11 A. R. Gaudreau (1680–1751). *Commode* with two drawers and gilt bronze mounts by J. Caffieri (1678–1755). Wallace Collection, London.

Probably made to a design by one of the five Slodtz brothers, three of whom worked as sculptors and designers at the Court, this *commode* is veneered with purplewood with borders of satinwood. It has two drawers at the front with keyhole escutcheons in the form of large leaves and two small cupboards at the sides. Lavish decoration in gilt bronze composed of scrolled branches and leaves covers the front and sides.

The piece stands on four curved legs of triangular section, ending in scroll feet with gilt bronze shoes. The top is of Levantine marble, basically green and white, flecked with red. The two small side cupboards are divided into compartments inside with cedarwood drawers.

12 *Console* table in gilded wood with dragons and masks. Musée des Arts Décoratifs, Paris.

13 Charles Cressent (1685–1768). *Commode*, probably made to a design of Nicolas Pineau (1684–1854). Wallace Collection, London.

This piece with its double curve was called *en arc d'arbalète* at the time. It is composed of two drawers decorated at the sides by two gilt bronze *espagnolettes*; gilt bronze mounts sheathe the legs and feet. An elegant motif incorporating dragons, shells, grapes and spirals covers the front, which is veneered with bright Cuban mahogany, purplewood and boxwood.

Charles Cressent, favourite cabinet-maker of the Regent, Philippe d'Orléans, worked in Paris from about 1714 and also worked for the Elector of Bavaria. His best works are preserved in the Louvre, in the *Cabinet des Médailles* and in the Wallace Collection in London.

14 Detail of the asymmetrical decoration of a drawer. A dragon curls around the escutcheon with spread wings and gaping jaws, its tail curved to form a handle for the top drawer. The handles of the bottom drawer are decorated with acanthus leaves. The gilt bronze decorations, somewhat reminiscent of the Louis XIV style, are thought to have been wrought by Cressent himself.

24

15

16

15 Charles Cressent. Cupboard with gilt bronze mounts. Musée des Arts Décoratifs, Paris.

This superb wardrobe made of purplewood is another piece by Charles Cressent. It is embellished with gilt bronze *appliqués* featuring allegorical figures closely resembling those used by Cressent on other pieces. In the eighteenth century the wardrobe was considered to be a piece of useful furniture and was generally relegated to the dressing-room: handsome wardrobes which had the honour of being displayed in public were rare indeed. Cressent probably worked on this piece about 1725–30.

16 The *Cabinet de la Pendule*, Versailles.

The magnificent carved wood decoration in the Clock Room is the work of Verbeckt who was active from 1738–60. The room took its name from the famous Passement clock, the work of Dauthiau and Caffieri; it was presented to the King in 1753 by the *Académie des Sciences*. The sumptuous gilt bronze case was made by Jacques Caffieri. The crystal ball which shows the phases of the sun, the moon and the planets follows the Copernican system, lower part bears a bronze sundial.

On the left of the room is a grey and violet marble fireplace, on which stands a bust of Louis XIV as a boy. In the centre of the room is a copy of an equestrian statue of Louis XV by Bouchardon. Above the doors are painted panels depicting pastoral scenes after Boucher, while beside the doors stands a splendid console table in carved and gilded wood with a frontal medallion and a fleur-de-lys motif.

17 *The Cabinet du Roi*. Versailles.

The King's room is one of the many salons in the apartments of Louis XIV. The massive silver furniture that used to fill the room was sacrificed by the Sun King for reasons of state, and was melted for the benefit of the national mint to meet war expenses. No thought was given to the works of art thus irrevocably destroyed. Later, Louis XV redecorated this and other salons.

17

18 A room in Louis XV's apartments, showing the famous *bureau à cylindre* started by J-F. Oeben (1710–1763) and completed by J-H. Riesener (1734–1806).

This bureau is an example of the work of two of the greatest French cabinet-makers. The exquisite workmanship of the panels inlaid with allegorical figures and the gilt bronze mounts make this a masterpiece. The roll-top (*à cylindre*) invented by Oeben himself, was operated by an ingenious mechanism, and was widely imitated in later years.

The upper part of the desk is enclosed by an ornate gallery, with solid bronze figures holding the candlesticks on each side. They were wrought by Duplessis and chased by Hervieu. Lepine made the double-faced clock set in the centre of the desk.

The piece was ordered from Oeben in 1761, but was not completed at his death. Riesener then completed it, putting his own signature on it.

19 Detail of the Bureau du Roi, made by J-F. Oeben and J-H. Riesener.

20 Council Room, Fontainebleau.
This room was completely redecorated by Louis XV. The panels are the work of Claude van Loo and J. B. Pierre, and are painted in pink and blue *camaïeu* (monochrome painting). It would be difficult to imagine a more frivolous decorative theme for this room, where decisions were frequently made about high level affairs of state. The panels with bunches of flowers and grotesques are the work of Alexis Payrotte.
The Louis XV style carpet and chairs were made from a design by Jacob Desmalter during the Empire. The candelabra wrought in gilt bronze by Galle belong to the same period (1807).

21 Council Room. Fontainebleau.
Detail of the fireplace, with two andirons embellished with pine cones and urns, standing on slender legs and surmounted by flames.

22 Drawing of a Louis XV chair. Note the curved lines of the back and legs, the scroll feet and the floral motif sketched in as a decoration.

22

23

23 E. Levasseur. Book-cabinet. Wallace Collection, London.
This is a large cabinet bookcase with three compartments, divided by ornamental panels in the form of pillars. The carcass of the bookcase is of oak: it is veneered with ebony and with marquetry of tortoiseshell and brass. The tops of the pillars are decorated with bearded masks flanked by acanthus leaves. The sides of the bookcase feature mythological scenes.
Each of the dividing panels conceals a small cupboard with three ebony shelves, each edged with brass. The escutcheons are embellished with eagle-head motifs, and the base of the piece has a gilt bronze moulding.
The inside of the bookcase is lined on both sides with violet velvet, with a mirror set in the back. On the back of the piece is the stamp 'E. Levasseur' repeated twice.
Etienne Levasseur probably used a design by Boulle for this piece; a similar bookcase can be seen in a painting at Versailles portraying the Monseigneur's study at Meudon. A pupil of Boulle, Levasseur won the title *Maître ébéniste* in April 1767; he specialized in repairing his master's furniture. Other works by Levasseur are at the Louvre, Fontainebleau and Versailles.

25 Jean Louis Faizelot Delorme (working c.1763–1780). Low bookcase. Wallace Collection, London.

The piece is divided into three sections, of which the central one bears a panel veneered with foliated marquetry of brass and tortoiseshell. In the centre is a figure of Pomona seated on a pedestal and flanked by musical instruments. The two lateral sections of the piece have glass doors, surrounded by exquisite brass inlay work of acanthus leaves, interspersed with gilt bronze keyhole escutcheons bearing eagle heads. The volute hinges are further embellished with foliations.

The base has a gilt bronze moulding and three rosettes; the central two of its six feet are squared while those at the four corners are circular, each surmounted by a gilt bronze capital.

Jean Louis Faizelot Delorme came from a family of cabinet-makers. Appointed *Maître ébéniste* in 1763, he soon adopted the signature 'JLFD', as distinct from his father who signed with his surname alone. The bronze mounts repeat Boulle's favourite motifs: they are to be found on a design for a cupboard by him which must date from about 1690.

26 Alexandre Fortier (working c.1725–60). Pendulum clock (second half of the eighteenth century). Wallace Collection, London.

This monumental clock with elaborate astronomical movement is enclosed in an ornate gilt bronze frame. The base is veneered with purplewood on oak, and is richly decorated with gilt bronze acanthus leaves, scrolls, ribbons and garlands. Under the central face is the signature of the clock-maker, Alexandre Fortier. A date, 1725, is scratched on one of the springs of the solar mechanism, but this may have come from an earlier clock.

The uppermost of the four dials gives Greenwich Mean Time, while below is a moving face on which is engraved a map of the world. The dial on the left gives the rising and setting of the sun, and that on the right the phases of the moon. The movement was invented by Fortier (working c.1725–60), and made by Michel Stollewerck (c.1746–75).

27 Nicholas Jean Marchand (c.1697–after 1757). *Commode*. Wallace Collection, London.

This fine piece is of oak veneer with ebony and has panels of black and gold lacquer. The lacquer on the front of the *commode* is probably European, but of oriental inspiration, while the side panels are presumed to be Japanese. The front and sides are *bombé* or convex in shape, and the front has a gilt bronze decoration in the form of acanthus leaves, which also forms the handles of the two drawers of the cabinet. The whole stands on four curved legs, which are triangular in section, and mounted at the feet with scrolled acanthus leaves. The top is of violet Breccia marble. Marchand's stamp appears twice on the bottom rail, at the back.

26

24 J. Baumhauer (died 1772). Cabinet. Wallace Collection, London

The doors of this low cabinet with three compartments are decorated with gilt bronze mythological figures in relief, set against panels of marquetry of brass and tortoiseshell. The framework is veneered with ebony. The central frieze at the top has a gilt bronze wave design, those at the sides with plumes alternating with acanthus leaves, while the base of the piece is bordered with gilt bronze mouldings and flanked by rosettes in the same metal. The compartments inside are of purplewood and have brass handles.

The piece is signed under the slab on the right with the name 'Joseph' between the two lilies. Experts have suggested that the piece could be the work of Gaspar Joseph Baumhauer, son of Joseph Baumhauer, and given the style of the friezes and inlays the attribution is likely enough. In any case, both father and son used to sign with their first name only. A chest with the same 'Joseph' stamp veneered with Japanese lacquer is at Windsor Castle, England, and shows some resemblance in form and ornament to this beautiful piece.

27

28

29   30

28 Antoine Gaudreau. Large *commode*. Versailles.

After a chequered history this *grande commode* is now once again in its rightful place in the *Cabinet du Roi* at Versailles. It was first delivered to Louis XV, who was a keen numismatist to contain his coin collection in 1729, and was made by Antoine Gaudreau, cabinet-maker to Louis XV for a quarter of a century. Inspired by the style of the Slodtz brothers, he favoured large areas of purple-wood parquetry and often decorated his pieces with chased and gilt bronze mounts worked by the Slodtz brothers themselves or by Caffieri.

29 G. Joubert (1689–1775). Corner cupboard. Versailles.

This piece was made to complement the *grande commode* (see 28) in Louis XV's *Cabinet du Roi*. The decoration of the corner cupboard closely resembles that of the *grande commode*, being decorated with medallions featuring allegorical figures, garlands and wreaths. Joubert was admitted as *Maître ébéniste* between 1717 and 1720.

30 Detail of the bronze medallion on the front of the corner cupboard.

31 Jean-Henri Riesener. *Commode*, veneered and inlaid with various woods. Versailles.

This is a typical piece by the famous eighteenth-century cabinet-maker. He worked, too, on the magnificent *Bureau du Roi* with its beautifully executed marquetry work. It is divided vertically into three sections, and horizontally into two drawers. On the central panel is an elegant decoration of flowers enclosed in an oval frame and surmounted by a gilt bronze escutcheon. The handles on either side are formed as escutcheons, surmounted by exquisitely made festoons of flowers. The feet are sheathed in gilt bronze acanthus leaves, the upper frieze has a rosette motif which runs along the three drawers, while rosettes and acanthus leaves decorate the angles.

32 F. Reizell (died 1788). Inlaid corner cupboard. Musée des Arts Décoratifs, Paris.

This is one of the few known pieces by this German cabinet-maker, who worked mainly in Paris, where he was employed by the Prince de Condé. This corner cupboard, one of Reizell's most important pieces, is inlaid in light woods on a dark chestnut ground. The central motif is formed of a bunch of carnations and roses tied with the traditional lover's knot. A gilt bronze frame in the *rocaille* style admirably sets off the rich colour effects obtained by contrasting the light woods with the darker chestnut.

35

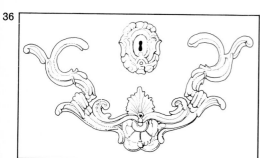

36

33 *Commode* in Chinese lacquer. Musée des Arts Décoratifs, Paris.

Louis XIV's cabinet-makers, exploiting the contemporary taste for Chinese lacquer, were content to apply to the carcases of their pieces lacquer panels brought from the East and depicting country scenes and pagodas. Later it became unnecessary to send to China for finished lacquer panels, because in 1748 the Martin brothers invented the famous *vernis Martin façon de Chine*. The oriental lacquer work can be easily distinguished from the rest by its black ground and gold designs. The Coromandel lacquers all portray people and are painted in bright colours.

34 Pierre Garnier (1720–1800). Lacquered *commode* with gilt bronze friezes. Musée des Arts Décoratifs, Paris.

The fashion for lacquered furniture was at its height at the end of the eighteenth century. The lacquer work on commodes and tables of all sizes was very similar, but the gilt bronze mounts differed in their themes and in their execution by artists of varying quality. This *commode* with two drawers had a

more compact design than the former (plate 33), the figures are well defined and the bronze decoration is more restrained. The works of Pierre Garnier, the Marquise de Mazarin's favourite cabinet-maker, cover the various changes in style from high rococo to the Directoire.

35 Claude Roumier. *Console* in sculpted and gilded wood. Versailles.

This is an important example of the work of Roumier, an ornamental sculptor who was a member of the Italian Accademia di San Luca. The *console* is in sculpted and gilded wood, incorporating a shield with three fleur-de-lys in the centre of the frieze; it was made for Versailles. Six years later Roumier made another, with the same crest of three lilies. It is not certain which is the earlier piece and there is little difference between them.

36 Drawing of a typical keyhole escutcheon and handle of gilt bronze in typical Louis XV style. The design in the form of shields or masks with inter-twined leaves and branches enabled the artist to use a variety of motifs.

37 Charles Topino. *Bonheur-du-jour.* Musée des Arts Décoratifs, Paris.

This elegant type of table, called a *bonheur-du-jour*, was very popular in the reign of Louis XV. It was a small table, usually with three legs (although the one illustrated has four), and it could be used as a work table, small desk or a dressing table. The legs were generally curved or fluted and nearly always strengthened by a stretcher. Sometimes one or more drawers would be set in the frieze. In this piece, designed by Topino, there is a central niche with doors on either side, and above a gallery of gilt bronze, another typical feature of these small pieces. Topino's marquetry features boxes, cups, and small urns worked in rare woods to give a *trompe-l'oeil* (three dimensional) effect. Few biographical details are known about Charles Topino, apart from the fact that he belonged to a group of *petits maîtres* that was active at the end of the eighteenth century. He worked until the Revolution and his pieces illustrate various styles.

38 Pierre Migeon II (1701–1758). *Commode à vantaux.* Musée des Arts Décoratifs, Paris.

This commode has two doors, which conceal the drawers. The profile is outlined by a simple gilt bronze strip of elegant fluting with an acanthus leaf motif at the corners. The marquetry work is of flowers executed in precious woods.

Migeon II was the son of a very famous cabinet-maker and he was fortunate enough to attract Madame de Pompadour's attention; after 1740 he could be numbered among the most fashionable cabinet-makers. The Migeon II style is essentially Louis XV, his pieces are superbly veneered often characterized by the addition of an outline in a darker wood instead of gilt bronze mounts. The signature 'Migeon' is often found on the pieces of both father and son.

37

38

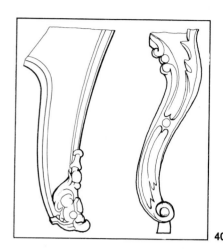

39 Jean-Baptiste Cresson (died 1781). A chair *à la reine*. Musée des Arts Décoratifs, Paris.

The chair is covered in fabric embroidered in *petit point* in turquoise on an ivory background. It suits the gay and capricious *rocaille* style of the frame particularly well.

The Cresson family, *menuisiers* of Paris numbered some ten masters among its members. All produced good work, but because they all signed with their surname without initials, they inadvertently caused much confusion and put the authenticity of some of their most important pieces in doubt. The cabinet-maker in chief, Jean-Baptiste, was active for about thirty years before XVI came to the throne.

40 A drawing of a cabriole leg ending in a scroll foot, and (left) a foot terminating in an acanthus leaf of gilt bronze.

41 Roger La Croix (Vandercreuse) (born 1727, worked until 1789). *Chiffonier*. Musée Nissim de Camondo, Paris.

This small elegant table, refined in line and harmonious in form is completely lacquered in yellow and maroon trellis work. The top is of Sèvres porcelain and matches the design of the table.

Roger Vandercreuse, better known as La Croix or Lacroix, was born of a Flemish family in Paris. He is among the most important cabinet-makers of the transitional period and was related to the top Parisian cabinet-makers' families; one of his sisters married J-F. Oeben then Jean-Henri Riesener. La Croix was appointed *Maître ébéniste* in 1755. He worked for the King, the Duc d'Orléans, and Madame du Barry, who valued his work highly. During the Revolution, he ceased all professional activity and worked only for his own pleasure. He signed himself R.V.L.C.

42

43

42 Roger La Croix. *Secrétaire à coulisse.* Musée des Arts Décoratifs, Paris.

The doors *à coulisse* of this original secrétaire open to reveal an interior amply furnished with niches and drawers for books and writing materials. The drawer below opens out to provide a writing surface, and the doors of the lower part of the piece conceal shelves which hold papers and books. The piece is completely veneered in rosewood, set in herringbone strips to allow the doors to run along the grooves. The escutcheons and tiny handles are in gilt bronze and do not distract the eye from the perfect veneer work. La Croix made much use of inlay, but used floral motifs, lacquer panels and porcelain plaques rarely, and then only in response to precise commissions from his clients. He was very restrained in his use of bronze mounts, employing them as little as possible and in simple form.

La Croix worked directly for the Court of Louis XV, the Dauphin and Madame Victoria. He was one of Marie-Antoinette's favourite cabinet-makers and his work was also highly regarded by her husband, Louis XVI.

43 The same piece with the doors closed.

44 Jean-Baptiste Tilliard (1685–1766). *Voyeuse* chair. Musée des Arts Décoratifs, Paris.

This type of chair was fashionable in France in the eighteenth century and is a variation of the *bergère*. Like the *bergère* it is completely upholstered, has short arms and a detachable cushion. The chief feature of this chair is its back, which is made of a little upholstered shelf, so that someone wishing to watch a game in progress at a card table can lean comfortably without disturbing the player. (The player would sit on the chair, with the observer leaning on the shelf and looking over his shoulder.)

Tilliard worked constantly for the French Court and was helped by his son, Jean-Baptiste II. He specialized in making sober and elegant seats and chairs.

45 Pierre Nogaret (1720–1771). Caned sofa. Musée Nissim de Camondo, Paris.

This sofa is part of a group of furniture for the drawing room which dates from 1750. The wooden frame and canework back belong to the late Regency or early Louis XV period. The frame is in polished walnut and is carved with rosettes and flowering branches: the back is divided into three, and the eight legs are slightly curved, elegant in line, and have scroll feet. The seat is upholstered in multi-coloured silk woven in one piece.

Nogaret, a native of Paris, preferred to work in the provinces, particularly in Lyons where he was employed by the *menuisier* Francois Girard. He remained a provincial cabinet-maker, as he proudly asserted whenever he could, stamping his pieces with the signature 'Nogaret à Lyons'.

44

45

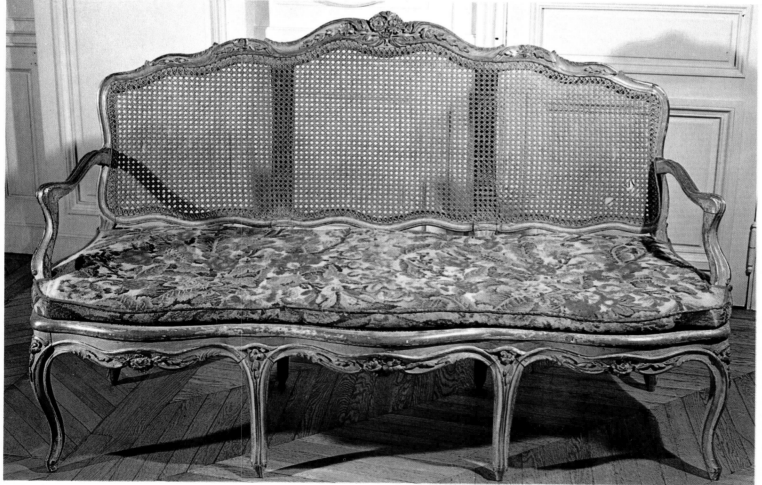

46 Charles Cressent. Cartel clock. Wallace Collection, London.

This typical wall clock in the rococo style was completed by the artist in 1747. The gilt bronze decorations, dominated by the sculptured figures of 'Love Triumphant' and 'Time' occupy the front of the piece, while the sides are worked in the Boulle style with brass and tortoiseshell. Surmounting it is the figure of Cupid, emerging from a cloud; he seems to bend his head down to gaze at Time, who in turn bends to meditate on Chaos, represented by the world. Behind the figure of Time is a trefoil-shaped space against which a sun in splendour is displayed: festoons, branched creepers and floral compositions encircle the face. On the back is the signature of various clock-makers who repaired the piece at different times.

There is a very similar clock in Windsor Castle, which incorporates a figure of Time resembling the one illustrated here. Charles Cressent, cabinet-maker to the Regent, Philippe d'Orléans, was the son of a sculptor and the grandson of the famous cabinet-maker. He learned the two arts from his father and grandfather but he is principally known as a cabinet-maker, although he personally wrought the bronze decorations for his pieces.

Although a law of 1723 prohibited cabinet-makers from decorating their furniture with bronzes not wrought by qualified *fondeurs* (founders), Cressent totally disregarded this rule and was often fined by the Tribunal du Chatelet for its infringement. On the death of the Regent, Cressent continued in the service of Louis XV. He was an avid collector of works of art, especially paintings, and it is said that he possessed an important collection of paintings by such famous artists as Raphael, Titian, Rubens and Holbein. However, in 1748 financial difficulties forced him to auction his collection. Nevertheless he kept back several works which he left to his housekeeper. Few pieces bear the Cressent signature, because only in his later years did he decide to sign the odd piece of minor importance.

47 48

47, 48 Jacques Verbeckt. *Boiseries*. Versailles.

The panelling in Versailles, with its sculpted and gilt detail against a white painted ground, was largely the work of Verbeckt. Those in the *Cabinet de la Pendule* in the dainty *rocaille* style are especially fine. While incorporating the usual motifs, Verbeckt's design maintains at the same time an elegance and simplicity of line in all its richly varied decorative themes.

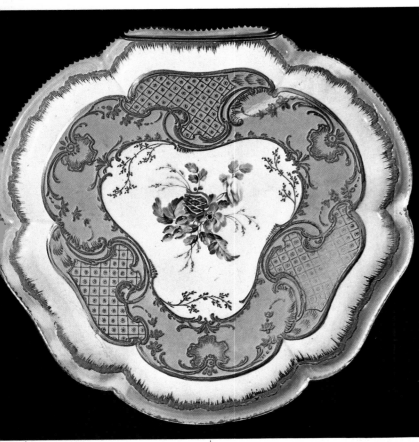

49 Large dish with floral decoration. Sèvres porcelain.

50 *Ecuelle* with two handles, lid and oval dish. Sèvres porcelain.

The Sèvres *Manufacture* was moved from Vincennes to Bellevue on the orders of Louis XV and Madame de Pompadour, so that it was only a few miles from Versailles. It was declared the property of the Crown, and the directorship was entrusted to Boileau, who had filled this office at Vincennes. Production was increased under the new management. Biscuit porcelain was developed with the use of hard paste, and particular attention was given to improving the standard of production, which was entrusted to well-known painters and modellers.

New colours for fine porcelain were developed and used: in 1757 the famous *rose Pompadour* was introduced in honour of Louis XV's favourite; later in 1763 the *bleu du Roi* was developed in honour of the sovereign. New shapes and new decorative motifs enriched the production of porcelain in the golden age of Sèvres. Commissions were received from all the reigning houses of Europe and from the aristocracy in many countries. The Revolution was a setback, and only later under the Directoire and during the Empire did the Sèvres porcelain factories regain their former greatness.

49

50

51

52

53

51 Claude Duvivier (second half of the eighteenth century). *Rocaille* candelabrum. Musée des Arts Décoratifs, Paris.

A typical example of the *rocaille* style, this ornate candelabrum was made in Paris in 1736 by the goldsmith Claude Duvivier after a design by Juste-Aurèle Meissonnier (Turin 1693–Paris 1750). A master sculptor and decorator of Italian origin, Meissonnier was granted the title of Designer and Goldsmith to the King by Louis XV, for his exceptional talents and the skill he displayed in developing the *rocaille* style.

52 Style of Thomas Germain (1673–c.1748). A pair of pot-pourri jars. Wallace Collection, London.

There are two identical Chinese jars in green celadon porcelain, enamelled in *famille rose* colours with floral designs in gold, with matching gilt mountings in the manner of Thomas Germain. They belong to the Ch'ien Lung period (1736–95), and both have a lid.

A gilt bronze openwork ring separates the jar and the lid, which has a knob in the form of a pomegranate. Shoots and vine leaves climb from the circular base to form two handles, complemented with acanthus leaves which form the four supporting feet. Thomas Germain, a Parisian by birth, was the son of Pierre Germain, Louis XIV's goldsmith. Thomas made articles in silver and gold for the aristocracy; he lived and worked at the Louvre where his best works are exhibited now.

53 Ewer in Meissen porcelain, in a mounting attributed to Jacques Caffieri. Wallace Collection, London.

This is one of the two existing examples of the Meissen Mayflower design. It has four reserved medallions painted in the Watteau style. The rococo mounting is in gilt bronze and the handle is modelled in the form of a bird with a long curved beak. It bears the Meissen mark of the period 1740–74. The number 104, which is impressed on the base, is probably that of the modeller. The ewer can be dated around 1749. A pair of similar but smaller ewers passed from the collection of Pierpont Morgan to the Cleveland Museum of Arts in Ohio in 1944.

54 The Queens' Bedroom. Fontainebleau.

This room is usually called the *Chambre des Reines* (the Queens' Bedroom), because it was used to accommodate the many consorts from the reign of Henri IV to that of Napoleon III. Marie de Médicis, wife of Henri IV, Marie-Thérèse, wife of Louis XIV, Marie Leszczynska, wife of Louis XV, Marie-Antoinette, wife of Louis XVI, Marie-Louise, Napoleon I's second wife, and Marie-Amélie, wife of Louis-Philippe, all slept here, in varying degrees of comfort, and the room came to be known as the 'room of the six Maries'. Marie-Antoinette's bed is kept here; the fabric that covers it is particularly sumptuous, woven in Lyons towards the end of Louis XVI's reign. The panel behind the bed belongs to the same period. The Empress Marie-Louise, wife of Napoleon I added the chairs at the foot of the bed. The room itself gives us some idea of interior decoration from the reign of Louis XVI to the end of the Empire.

55 The Rousseau brothers. Marie-Antoinette's Boudoir (1785). Fontainebleau.

The pale green walls are decorated with arabesque in the Pompeian style made popular by the excavations of the time. The boudoir contains the magnificent *bureau à cylindre*, made by Jean-Henri Riesener, with its beautiful marquetry of mother-of-pearl, silver and bronze. There is also an elegant work-table with lyre legs and tray top en suite with the desk using mother-of-pearl, gilt bronze and silver.

56

57

56 Louis XVI's Library. Versailles.

The room, designed by Jacques-Ange Gabriel, was executed by Antoine Rousseau. It is completely lined with bookcases, divided by inlaid pillars. Panels depicting allegorical scenes are placed in the corners, and marble busts of the Roman Emperors are arranged on the cornices of the bookcases. A large sequoia wood table is placed in the middle of the room; it was made by Roentgen (1743–1793). A large carpet woven with the fleur-de-lys design is spread on the floor, and chairs *à la reine* are arranged around the walls.

57 The Queen's Gaming Room. Fontainebleau.

The decorative wall panels adorned with stucco and with painted Pompeian candelabrum designs are the work of the Rousseau brothers. The same motif is repeated around the doors.

Two fine *commodes* are placed against the walls; these pieces are richly decorated with gilt bronze and Sèvres plaques. The screen is covered in flowered satin; the pattern was copied at a later period for the fabric covering the firescreen and the chairs which line the walls. The tables for playing backgammon and card games are placed in the middle of the room, and are in the Louis XVI style. The marble clock portraying Sappho, is however, in the Empire style; it is the only hint that we are given that the room was changed by Joséphine Bonaparte from a gaming room to a music room.

58 *Cabinet de la Méridienne.* Versailles.

This room, designed for the Queen's afternoon repose, was completed in 1781. The *boiseries* (panelling), decorated with foliate borders are the work of the Rousseau brothers, and the carved frames of the mirrors are a fine example of Fortier's work. A gilt wooden chair with a draped back and scroll feet upholstered in pale blue velvet matches the curtains. The central table is inlaid with metals.

59 *Oeil de Boeuf* salon. Versailles.

This room owes its name to the oval aperture above the fireplace. It has not been altered since the time of Louis XIV, when it was used as an ante-room where courtiers would gather before being admitted to the King's robing. The stucco frieze on a trellis-work gold ground portrays children at play. Many painters worked on the decoration of this room, from Van Clève to Poirer. The bust of Louis XIV, on the fireplace, is the work of Coysevox, the sculptor of the beautiful nymph in the Palace gardens.

58

59

60 Jean-Henri Riesener. *Commode.* Wallace Collection, London.

The *commode* is in three sections and has concave sides, which are an unusual feature of this magnificent oak piece. It is veneered with an interlinking diamond motif with inlays in various woods, the frieze is of gilt bronze and the top is in *verts des Alpes* marble. The *commode* stands on four fluted feet enriched with bronze scrolls and acanthus leaves. The frieze that conceals the drawers is veneered in sycamore and decorated with flowering branches of roses and lilies in gilt bronze. Narcissi encircle the keyholes and the handles are in the form of gilt bronze leaves. The plaque on the central door is inlaid with a trophy of musical instruments. The angles of the concave sides are decorated with gilt bronze floral pendants.

61 Jean-Henri Riesener. *Secrétaire en abattants.* Wallace Collection, London.

This *secrétaire* is tall and square with fall-top flap in the upper part and two doors below. In the centre is an oval plaque of chased and gilt bronze portraying a scarifice to Cupid, while on the angles are pilasters to which are attached brackets from which pendants of gilt bronze flowers fall. The base is decorated with a motif of cornucopias and garlands. The top is of Carrara marble. Inside, the drawers and flaps are lined with blue leather.

The back bears the mark 'JHR', partly rubbed out, and on the central panel can be seen the initials CT, surmounted by a crown. The bronze decorations are in the style of Gouthière, and the plaques are reminiscent of the style of Claude Michel, also known as Clodion (1738–1814). Official documents show that the piece was built for the Queen, and was placed in the Palace of Versailles. The piece, in fact, is inlaid with Marie-Antoinette's favourite marquetry design. A similar *secrétaire*, also built for the Queen by the same cabinet-maker, is now in the Frick Collection in New York and was made about 1790.

62   Jean-Francois Leleu (1729–1807). *Bureau en abattant*. Musée Nissim de Camondo, Paris.

The bureau is decorated with marquetry, of hexagonal shapes enclosing rose-wood rosettes, and has a gilt bronze frieze. At each end of the upper panel is a gilt bronze rosette. The small cupboard underneath has four drawers.

Jean-Francois Leleu began his career under the eye of Oeben, and was one of the most prolific cabinet-makers in the style of Louis XVI. Initially he worked for Madame du Barry and later for Marie-Antoinette. His signature was a scroll bearing the initials JFL.

63   Martin Carlin (died 1785). *Guéridon*. Musée Nissim de Camondo, Paris.

This mahogany *guéridon*, rich in gilt and chased bronze, has three legs in the form of twin colonettes of gilt bronze which rest on a triangular base with curved feet. A small tray is set on a bronze stem in the centre of the triangular base. A writing drawer is concealed in the frieze. The top is of Siena marble.

64   Adam Weisweiler. *Commode d'appui*. Musée Nissim de Camondo, Paris.

Veneered with ebony and Japanese lacquer, this elegant piece is one of a pair, both bearing the signature AW. There is a single door and one decorative vase motif in gold on a black ground, enclosed in a gilt bronze frame. The top is in Spanish broccatello marble. Weisweiler's style, with its widespread use of Japanese lacquer and Sèvres porcelain medallions for decoration is typical of the end of Louis XVI's reign.

65 Jean-Henri Riesener. *Commode d'appui*. Musée Nissim de Camondo, Paris.
   This is a richly inlaid piece, divided into three parts. The two side ones open into two drawers, and the central cupboard with two doors is inlaid with a floral bouquet of rare woods. The inlay on the side panels is formed of shallow lozenges placed horizontally. Above are three drawers, concealed with a beautiful gilt bronze frieze. Brackets from which fall pendants of acanthus foliage decorate the corners. The edge moulding on the lower part of the piece develops into a luxurious leaf design.

66 Drawing of a decoration for gilt bronze work.
   This motif was greatly favoured by the cabinet-makers of the late eighteenth century.

65

66

67 René Dubois (1737–1799). *Commode en console*. Wallace Collection, London.

This piece is sometimes known as Marie-Antoinette's wedding chest. It stands on tall fluted legs resting on twisted gilt bronze feet with spiral flutes, and has a large drawer at the front and a cupboard at each end. It is covered with European and Japanese lacquer beneath a fretted mount of pseudo-Oriental inspiration. Caryatids representing four sirens with twisted tails grace the corners, each one bearing on its head a cushion from the corners of which garlands of flowers fall. In the middle of the front is a lacquer panel to which are applied two kissing doves of gilt bronze; they are enclosed in a gilt bronze oval frame surmounted by a lion's mask. A delightful wreath of flowers runs along the edge of the base. The central and side drawers are lined in pink silk. The monogram G. Dubois is imprinted on the Breccia marble top.

Tradition has it that the piece was made as a wedding coffer for Marie-Antoinette but there is no documentary evidence to support this. It was probably repaired by Vitel towards the middle of the nineteenth century; the caryatid sirens are attributed to Maurice Falconet (1716–1791).

68 Detail of the gilt bronze caryatid sirens, attributed to Falconet.

69 Voyeuse chair in carved wood covered in red velvet.

This *voyeuse*, without arms (unlike the one illustrated in plate 44), allowed its user to sit astride, if he so wished.

70 Claude Charles Saunier (1735–1807). Low bookcases. Musée Nissim de Camondo, Paris.

This very simple low bookcase in mahogany, decorated in chased and gilt bronze, has two glass doors underneath an ornate frieze. Small caryatids adorn the angles, and the top is of white marble. Claude Charles Saunier is the most representative of a whole school of cabinet-makers active under Louis XV. Appointed *Maître* in 1752, he only started to sign his works around 1765. His marquetry decoration is usually composed of rosewood and ebony, often complemented with *vernis Martin*. At the end of his career the artist seemed to prefer simpler furniture with light bronze decorations.

69

70

71 Jean-Francois Leleu or Martin Carlin. Cabinet with drawers and Sèvres porcelain plaques. Wallace Collection, London.

This piece is in two sections, the upper part having two doors surmounted by a clock set in a moulded plinth and case of gilt bronze. Two candlesticks are affixed to each side by acanthus branches. The veneer is of tulip wood on oak. The upper cupboard has an apple-green Sèvres plaque with a floral design in the centre of each drawer. The drawers and doors of the lower part are mounted with square tiles in Sèvres porcelain of the same colour.

The signature Julien Le Roy can be seen under the clock face, while below the plinth on the right is that of Jean-Francois Leleu. On the lower part of the piece the signature of Martin Carlin can still be seen, despite attempts to rub it out. The piece has undergone many restorations and alterations; it was probably made by Leleu and repaired at a later date, by Martin Carlin. Alternatively, the latter could have made the piece and Leleu restored it.

72 Martin Carlin. *Secrétaire*. Wallace Collection, London.

Bow-shaped with a fall front, the *secrétaire* is set with a circular plaque of Sèvres porcelain and flanked by three open, bow fronted shelves in a curved recess, each with a gilt bronze gallery. At the top is a drawer decorated with swags in gilt bronze. Under the fall front is a drawer with a highly original moulding. The plaques, all of Sèvres porcelain, are in pale green which sets off the colourful bunches of flowers; they are enclosed in gilt bronze mouldings. Behind the fall-flap are fine pigeon-holes and six drawers surrounding another pigeon-hole. The faces of the drawers are veneered with tulipwood inlaid with fillets of boxwood and ebony. Gilt bronze shells act as handles. The drawers are lined in green velvet and the inside of the door is rose-coloured velvet edged with tulipwood and boxwood stringing. The porcelain plaques bare the initials MC, probably those of the painter Commelin (1768–1802).

73 Martin Carlin. Reading stand. Wallace Collection, London.

This light and graceful little table has a movable top which can be raised on a ratchet to make a comfortable reading stand. The top and four sides are of Sèvres porcelain painted with baskets of flowers. When the top is lifted the piece reveals a shallow trap, which serves as a top to the table when the reading stand is open.

Little is known about the life of Martin Carlin, except that he learned his craft in Oeben's studio. Oeben owed him five hundred francs when he died, and left him some valuable pieces, in payment. Carlin favoured Sèvres porcelain inserts, but also used Japanese lacquer.

74 Head of a ram.

This decorative motif was used in furniture of the Louis XVI style together with winged sphinxes, caryatids, acanthus leaves and interlaced ribbons.

73
74

72

54

75 Jean-Francois Leleu. *Secrétaire*. Musée des Arts Décoratifs, Paris.

This small piece – shaped almost like a 'cello – and the decorations that embellish it, are in pure Louis XV style. The fall-top flap and the door below are inlaid with Chinese lacquer panels featuring gold and red figures on a black ground. The mounts are of gilt bronze with delicate pendants of flowers, cartouches, and acanthus leaves at the corners. Furniture made in the Louis XV style is exceptional in the work of this cabinet-maker, who was one of Oeben's best pupils and who strove to attain a severe and simple classicism.

76 Adam Weisweiler. *Console-buffet*. Musée Nissim de Camondo, Paris.

This elegant *console* for the dining room is in mahogany chased and decorated with gilt bronze. The glass at the back sets off the two white marble shelves, whose corners are rounded. They are supported by fluted columns and each shelf is edged with a gallery. The top is in white marble, supported by a rich frieze in gilt bronze.

77

78

77 Claude Charles Saunier. *Secrétaire à cylindre.* Musée Nissim de Camondo, Paris.

Taking the famous *bureau du Roi* by Oeben and Riesener as a model, the French cabinet-makers, especially Saunier, devoted their activities to producing other forms of the genre. This roll-top desk dates from about 1775–85. It is made of *moucheté* (plum-pudding) mahogany, with three drawers at the top and five below as well as those set in the side. The gilt bronze mounts are very restrained, featuring interlaced branches, frets, and delicate beading. The top drawers have shield-shaped keyhole escutcheons and the lower ones have ring handles. A shelf can be pulled out from each side of the desk to act as a rest for books and papers. The desk stands on four fluted legs, each decorated with gilt husk pendants.

78 Jean-Henri Riesener. *Bureau à cylindre* in mahogany. Musée des Arts Décoratifs, Paris.

Here is a smaller version of the great *bureau à cylindre* (roll top desk) built for Louis XV by the famous cabinet-maker. This version is in polished mahogany with a series of drawers along the top and inside the *cylindre*. There is no decoration apart from the little masks on the keyhole escutcheons and drawer handles. The piece stands on tall, fluted legs which enhance its simple elegance.

79 Arm chair. Musée Nissim de Camondo, Paris.

The frame of this chair is carved in various designs and a spiral ribbon ornament covers the back and seat frame. There are overlapping scales and acanthus leaves on the arm supports. The legs are fluted, and the whole surface is gilt. The arm chair is upholstered with tapestry.

80 Etienne Avril. Small cupboard. Fontainebleau.

This piece now stands in the Queens' bedroom, but it may have been part of the furnishings of the Palace of Saint-Cloud. Certainly it was made by Etienne Avril for Marie-Antoinette. The simple lines of the little cupboard and the striking contrast between the bright blue medallions in Sèvres porcelain and the sombre hue of the mahogany, framed only by delicate gilt bronze borders make this work a masterpiece of simple elegance and good taste.

79

80

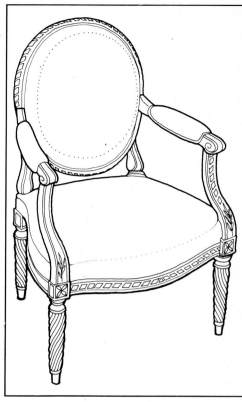

81

82

81, 82 Two *pliants* covered in red velvet with gold embroidery and fringes.

This type of *tabouret* (stool) with crossed carved legs was much in vogue during Louis XIV's reign, being designed for the use of courtiers of second rank who were not permitted to use chairs. Later, the *tabouret* became a widely used piece of furniture; it was an indispensable part of the furnishings for ballrooms, galleries and salons. Another type of stool with legs in the shape of two semicircles became popular in the Napoleonic era.

83 Drawing of a chair.

J-B. Lelarge (1743–1802) made many like this under Louis XVI and the Directoire. Medallion-back chairs, also referred as *à l'Artois*, had barley-sugar turned legs, and frames carved with ribbons and flowers, and are typical of this period.

84 Jean Ferdinand Schwerdferger. Large jewel chest. Versailles.

This piece was presented to Marie-Antoinette by the city of Paris, and the formal lines give a hint of the Empire style to come: it is a monumental piece resting on eight legs in the form of quivers which are enclosed within rich gilt bronze decoration. The caryatids representing the seasons were probably wrought by Thomire (1751–1783). The chest is inlaid with mother-of-pearl, glass, painted panels of grotesques by Degault and plaques in white and blue Sèvres porcelain rather like English Wedgwood. At the top of the piece is a group of allegorical figures which originally bore the Royal Crown.

85 Pierre Joseph Gouthière (1732–c.1813). Cartel clock, known as the Avignon Clock. Wallace Collection, London.

This clock, made of gilt bronze, part burnished, part matt, has the dial supported by two eagles, white symbolic figures are grouped around representing the city of Avignon and the two rivers, the Rhône and the Durance. The figures are arranged on a rocky base supported on a red Levantine marble plinth. The clock dial is the work of N. P. Delunes.

The complex allegorical motif refers to the cession of the city of Avignon by Pope Clement XIII to Jean Louis de Rochouart in 1768, representing the French King Louis XV. The new governor was extremely popular with the townsfolk, who presented him with this clock in December 1771. The chasing is the work of Gouthière, and is another example of the superlative craftsmanship that is also seen in the pieces he made for Fontainebleau.

86 Du Tertre. Cartel barometer. Musée des Arts Décoratifs, Paris.

After Louis XV's reign, *régulateurs* or barometers could be found in every room in the royal apartments. The Cartel type, still fashionable in Louis XVI's reign, was adorned with friezes and ribbons. Most of them were topped by an urn or tripod from which garlands and ribbons would fall in profusion around and face. Du Tertre was one of the most active bronze chasers of his time.

85   86

87 Gabriel Gerbu (working at the end of the eighteenth century). Three-branched candlestick. Musée des Arts Décoratifs, Paris.

Very simple in line, the decorative motifs of pendant swags and garlands of flowers are particularly elegant. The floral motif is repeated in chiselled detail on the stem.

88 Robert Joseph Auguste. Sauce tureen with dish and spoon. Musée Nissim de Camondo, Paris.

This sauce tureen stands on a dish of chased silver; it is decorated with medallions in relief, surrounded by oak leaves and surmounted by a coronet. The lid has a bear's head handle set over a group of oak leaves, while the four feet of the bowl are formed as acanthus leaves. The shell-shaped spoon bears on the handle the same marquis' coronet as can be seen on the bowl. It bears the mark of Robert Joseph Auguste and the date letter for 1784–5.

89 Jacques Nicolas Roettier (working 1765–1784). Tureen in chased silver with circular base. Musée Nissim de Camondo, Paris.

The finely chased bowl bears a circlet of laurel leaves which form the two handles; the cover has a chased oval knob, and the four feet are scroll shaped. The back, chiselled with radiating plates is supported by eight peg-top feet.

The tureen is part of a huge service made for Catherine the Great of Russia, who gave it to Count Orloff. On his death, the service reverted to the possession of the Empress. In the Metropolitan Museum in New York there is a soup tureen which was also part of this service.

87

88   89

90

91

90 *Applique.* Musée Nissim de Camondo, Paris.
This *applique*, is chased and gilt bronze, wrought in the shape of acanthus leaves, is typical of the eighteenth century, and can be dated between 1770 and 1780.

91 Pair of four-branched candelabra in gilt bronze. After Pierre Gouthière. Wallace Collection, London.
The two candelabra are set on an ovoid base in blue enamel with decorative bands of grapes and festoons of flowers. Each divides into four branches which spring from a central stem in the form of a torch. The central band bears moulded female heads on either side, while the urn rests on a square gilt bronze base. The style of craftsmanship resembles that of Gouthière, the design being reminiscent of Louis Simon Borzot (1743–1805). A similar candelabrum, but with a crystal bowl instead of an enamel one, is in Paris in the Musée Nissim de Camondo.

92

93

94

92 Le Riche (1743–1809). A group in Sèvres hard biscuit. Musée Nissim de Camondo, Paris.

The piece is called 'Love about to pounce'. It is a biscuit figurine, one of a series called the 'Three Naked Cupids'.

93 L.C. Boizot (1743–1809). Musée Nissim de Camondo, Paris.

This group is called 'A Gift to Love', and is part of the series 'Beauty Crowned by the Graces', completed in 1776. The blue base is decorated with chased bronze garlands.

94 F.N. Menière. Candlesticks in chased and gilt bronze. Musée Nissim de Camondo, Paris.

The two candlesticks have concave bases, cast and chased with radiating flutes. Around the stem are four finely chased garlands. Menière was appointed *Maître orfèvre* in November 1770, and the candlesticks here bear the maker's mark with the date letter for 1772–3.

95
96

95 Louis Falconet. Screen with six panels. Musée Nissim de Camondo, Paris.
This double-sided screen in pink silk surrounded by a fine embroidered border has a light carved wooden frame. The design features rushes and leaves above, and bunches of roses below. The other side is covered in a design of bunches of white roses. Louis Falconet was appointed *Maître ébéniste* in 1743.

96 Georges Jacob. Firescreen. Musée Nissim de Camondo, Paris.
This firescreen is made of mahogany with a fluted frame and silk panels striped in white, blue and yellow. It bears the stamp of Georges Jacob, who worked for Louis XV and XVI, and also under the Directoire and the Empire. His stamp bears his initial separated from his surname by a cross.